AF656064

Sadhus & Shamans

मेला

A sadhu sorts out his dreadlocks, which are a sign of his realisation of the unimportance of appearances, as well as his commitment to the spiritual life.

Preceding pages: Sadhus taking out a procession.

Sadhus & Shamans

Swati Chopra

Lustre Press
Roli Books

CONTENTS

Facing page: A shaman during a divination ritual. Following pages: A gathering of sadhus; they are renouncers who have chosen to live a life which is focused on their own spiritual practice.

भैरव मेडिकल्स

INTRODUCTION

Mystic Men of the East

An Indian sadhu, not quite equivalent to monks found elsewhere in the world, is a free-spirited wanderer who has cut his or her ties with worldly relationships and has set off on a quest.

Facing page: A shaman standing in a lake atop a boulder, performing what is possibly a divination ritual.

The wisdom traditions of Asia, and particularly of the Indian subcontinent, are originators of some of the most interesting and varied models of spiritual seeking in the history of humankind. One such model is that of the sadhu, which does not quite fit into the equivalent model of the monk or monastic found elsewhere in the world. A sadhu can be a free-spirited wanderer, who has cut his or her ties with worldly relationships and has set off, penniless and homeless, on a quest. What this quest is, what it entails, and what it aims to achieve, will form a crucial part of this book.

A sadhu can also be part of an organised monastic system, in which case he is nested within a community that takes care of his needs, provides a place to stay, and there also might be guidance available, for one looking to engage in serious spiritual 'sadhana' (practice), in the form of teachers and gurus. The community can also be an enabling space for the spiritual seeker, helping fulfil not just material needs but by providing a support system which might be crucial in the absence of family, and other conventional support systems that the seeker has left behind.

Monastic organisations can exist within the purview of organised religions, as is the case with sects that exist within the Hindu, Jain and Buddhist faiths, or they can spring up around individual teachers and gurus, and grow into full-fledged monastic sects with the passage of time. It is interesting to note that the latter phenomenon might, in time, metamorphose into the former. The group that forms around a charismatic teacher, might, in time, take on the contours of a religion. The ready example from the Indian subcontinent that comes to mind is the Buddha, whose solitary quest for truth gave birth to an entire religion that has adherents in several parts of Asia today.

Since we are looking at monasticism in the Indian context, we also need to examine the role, factors like gender and caste play, in the lives of sadhus. This is especially relevant because these are the two parameters that have been used

The naga sadhu is a seemingly esoteric feature in the akhara system of monastic organisation. The nagas make public appearance only during the Kumbh and Mahakumbh Melas. They have a martial past, and even today might train in the use of weapons and the arts of war.

A sadhu dries his loincloth after a ritual bath in the Ganga. Sadhus congregate on the banks of the holy river on auspicious occasions when bathing in her waters is considered especially beneficial.

Facing page: A shaman lights incense in a burner, possibly at the beginning of a ritual, in the ancient city of Bukhara in Uzbekistan.

to deny access to sacred knowledge traditionally, and because sadhus have often been able to take advantage of the unbounded nature of their existence to query taboos, related to caste and gender, in traditional society. Sadhus at times have also occupied a place of social activist, who uses spiritual truths in the cause of bettering society and showing up its follies. The Bauls of Bengal is one such tradition of wandering sadhus that use their music and poetry to hold up a mirror to society, and nudge it towards a path richer in values than traditional mores.

On the surface, it might appear as if sadhus and shamans belong to opposite ends of the spectrum, with the latter fulfilling a particular role in society, while the sadhu is quite outside society, on his own trip. And yet, both are truth-seekers in their own ways. The sadhu sets off on his own journey to find the truth, not content with version he has been given by others, and would like to find out things for himself. The shaman, too, is attempting to connect with a truth – that of a happening, or a person, or an illness, or a 'spirit'. While the extent of their journeys and the levels of the truth they seek might differ, both sadhus and shamans are looking for a connection with a level of reality not apparent on the surface.

Shamans essay a range of roles in societies that customarily consult them. They might be diviners, soothsayers, oracles, exorcists, talisman-makers, faith healers, and sometimes healers who use traditional healing methods and recipes with herbs and spices. At the best, they can be connectors with an alternative vision of reality; at their worst, they can turn out to be fakes and charlatans.

In the Himalayas, shamans are plentiful and are often consulted to dispense remedies, and suggest solutions to vexatious problems. Bon, the pre-Buddhism

Three sadhus race down the steps of a ghat for a ritual bath. The one who leads draws out a sword, and possibly belongs to a martial akhara.

Facing page: A naked sadhu with a dreadlocked beard catches up with the news, it seems. Renunciation of home and family might not mean complete disinterest in worldly matters, as is evident from this photograph.

Following pages: There are 4-5 million sadhus in India, widely respected for their holiness.

religion of Tibet, is especially rich in shamanistic practices, having sprung in a land of long winters, short days, and in pre-industrial times,and a limited contact with the outside world. A landscape populated with ghosts and spirits was imagined into being, and shamanistic practices devised to control them as well as communicate with them across the trans-Himalayan region. The south of India, too, has robust shamanistic traditions, like Bhuta Kola of Karnataka and Theyyam of Kerala, which rely on the spirits of deities for creating a psycho-drama in which the believers become willing participants.

Here, then, are the sadhus and shamans of the Indian subcontinent. Through a collection of unusual and candid photographs, their worlds are brought into being before our eyes, even as we begin to see the common strands that bind them, and us, into a complex whole.

Celebrating
the joy

SEEKERS OF TRUTH

The Devotion of Sadhus

A sadhu smoking his chillum, a conical pipe made of clay and used for the ritual intake of opiates like hashish and ganja, beloved to the Hindu god, Shiva.

Facing page: Naga sadhus smeared with ash, usually taken from funeral pyres. The intention behind this seemingly ghoulish ritual is to keep the knowledge of death close, and to strengthen one's resolve to devote oneself to spiritual practice alone.

Literally, the term 'sadhu' derives from the Sanskrit word, sadhana, which refers to the practice of something with complete dedication and a single-pointed focus to the exclusion of all else. A sadhu is one who engages in sadhana, while 'sadhvi' is the feminine form of the term sadhu. Usually the term sadhana is used for spiritual practice, though the meaning is not implied in a strict translation of the term. Sadhana could be used for intense engagement of any kind – in music, studies, writing a book, and so on – provided it is done with the intention of honing and deepening whatever one is doing.

Embedded in the term 'sadhu' is another meaning besides spiritual engagement,that of renunciation. The systems and models might differ from one sect of monasticism to another, or it might be a free-flow the individual is in, but a common factor in all is of sannyas, or renunciation. It is an understanding the individual comes to – that the ties that bind him to home, family, community, and in a sense caste and creed too, need to be severed, so he or she can become completely free to pursue the sadhana demanded by a spiritual quest.

THE ADVENTURE BEGINS

The act of renunciation can be seen as the beginning of a spiritual adventure. The nest of family, home and community that we are born into provides us with a sense of identity, of who we are. These form our natural comfort zones, where we are accepted, held, taken care of. Most of us spend our entire lives in the warmth of this nest, strengthening it and adding to it our own families in due course. In India, where social and familial bonds are strong and play a significant role in determining our self-worth and a sense of who we are, this nest is even more central to people's lives. It is also a net of relationships that provides not just comfort; it also requires a certain degree of adherence to tradition, to what has been done, and what is considered the 'right' way of doing things. When we choose to remain within their purview, we also acquiesce to this diktat – that

A band of barefooted sadhus. The tradition of the wandering sadhu is a time-honoured one in India. Some believe it is as old as the history of civilization in the subcontinent, and can be dated back to the Indus Valley Civilization around the fourth century BCE.

Facing page: A sadhu relaxes in his tent with a western devotee. With the growing appreciation for Indian spirituality, sadhus have attracted seekers from around the world curious for a glimpse into their lifestyles, disciplines and practices.

we will live our lives along accepted and acceptable patterns, and attempt to harmonise ourselves with other aspects of the nest as much as possible.

While this might be useful in terms of having a structure upon which the edifice of society and culture are built, and India has a continuous one several thousand years old, it can be a major roadblock in the path of the spiritual quest. Why is this so?

The spiritual quest must begin by learning to look within, understanding the identity that we have built about ourselves, and deconstructing it brick by brick. The reason for this is that the identity that we think we are, which includes the body, mind and the ego-personality, is understood in spirituality as being merely a façade. It is a veil upon our true self. When we can realize that there is an aspect of us, that underlies what we usually experience as our personality, that has to do with consciousness rather than the mind-body continuum we mostly spend our time being, we begin to get a glimpse of what this true self might be.

To even begin this journey within requires a tremendous resolve, because as is evident, it is not easy to look beyond the structures of our ego-personality. We have always believed – this is who I am. So it is impossible to veer away from this belief in a day or two. We might get it intellectually, but to actually realize it requires a different practice and commitment, which for some might begin with the act of renunciation. This is an act that is structured towards enabling us to unlearn whatever we have learnt in the course of our lives. It can be seen as wiping the slate clean and beginning afresh, this time with a radically

A striking photograph of a solitary sadhu, with his meagre belongings packed in a small bag, the sum total of what he owns. He is, as if ready to take off on yet another pilgrimage, which is considered to be an outward manifestation of the inner journey the sadhu is committed to.

different orientation. At the level of everyday reality, in the act of becoming a sadhu one must divest oneself of relationships, home and family and all material possessions. Thereafter, nothing will be owned, and the only possessions a sadhu will have will be the barest of necessities.

Above and facing page: In both these photographs sadhus perform austerities, each of which have a specific yogic purpose, but to the untrained eye are little more than exotic oddities, much like the popular image of the yogi sleeping on a bed of nails. The sadhu on the facing page is, in fact, lying on thorns, his skin pierced with needles.

Most sadhus will, at the time of renunciation, be given a new name that reflects their spiritual resolve. Depending on their order or guru, these might range from names of deities like Krishna, Shiva and so on, to states of being that are identified with the spiritual quest, like 'Atmananda' (the bliss of atman), and so on. They also acquire the honorific 'swami', which literally means, 'one who is master of himself'. Though the mastery might come in the course of their lives, the idea is perhaps to start off on a good note and hand the aspirant a credible goal to work towards.

Along with a new name and the robes of the order he or she has been inducted in, most Hindu orders give the aspirant a mantra to start with. They are supposed to 'japa' (recite) this mantra as often as possible, turning it on the rosary of their breath if possible. Then there are the vows – disciplines – that the sadhu commits himself to, all of which will be dealt with in detail later in the book. Sometimes, if the sadhu is also joining an order of monastics, he is inducted as a novitiate at the same ceremony.

DEEP IMPACT

The whole point of having an individual undergo these changes is to impress upon the psyche the beginning of a process of unlearning, which must be accompanied by a new way of looking at and thinking of, by oneself. So a cutting of ties with

Naga sadhus in an exuberant mood at a Kumbh Mela. Feared for their unpredictable nature, clashes are frequent among nagas of rival akharas, many of whom also carry weapons.

Facing page: A sadhu seated in the full lotus position – the padmasana – considered to be the ideal asana for entering deep states of meditation, which this sadhu seems to be in.

Following pages: Sadhus engage in a vast variety of religious practices, ranging from asceticism to praying and meditation.

family and friends means that one has opted out of the old way of being and is now ready to explore another. The vow of celibacy has at its heart a resolve to disengage from the drama of sexuality and the emotionality that is attached to it.

The giving up of possessions indicates a move towards a non-materialistic attitude to life. Wanting and grasping is inherent in the nature of materiality. Often, the human being is a poor judge of his own needs and wants and mistakes the latter for the former. Does one really need another pair of jeans, or does one merely want it? In the present atmosphere of unbridled consumerism and materialism, greed is seen as being a desirable emotion because if one wants more, one will buy more, and so keep the wheels of the economy turning.

The points that are missed in this celebration of greed is the kind of mental state it creates when it arises – one of grasping and craving, which makes for a mind that is restless and not at peace. Then, if the desire is fulfilled it is no guarantee that a fresh desire will not supplant it almost immediately, forming a vicious cycle in which one is constantly revolving from one desire to another, the fulfilment of these being incidental to the process of the arousal of further desires. And if a desire is not fulfilled, as will happen a lot of times, then the mind becomes a battleground besieged by frustration and sorrow. Either way, the individual suffers.

This is a primary reason for cutting out all the likely sources of desires in the process of accepting sannyas – money, possessions, home, job and also relationships, which are potent and perhaps the most insistent sources of desire. Expectations accompany human love in any relationship, whether it is that of a wife and a husband, a child with parents, of siblings, with in-laws, even with most friends. There is an unsaid quid pro quo in operation, and when even the least of the expectations with loved ones is not met in the way one would like it to be, the result is frustration and sadness. Again, there is suffering.

Bata

TATA
indicom
TRUE PAID
बादल ठंडई
THANDAI
BANK ATM
भारतीय स्टेट बैंक
State Bank Of India

A sadhu buried in the ground, with only his face and dreadlocks visible, offers a strange spectacle to onlookers who have offered him some coins, as a token of recognition of his holiness.

Facing page: A sadhu swamped with strings of rudraksha, a seed derived from the tree Elaeocarpus Ganitrus, and considered especially appropriate for making rosaries.

To engage in the spiritual quest, one needs to understand these interrelationships within us, and their impact on our behaviour and state of being. Only then can one actually begin to take them off, so to speak, like soiled clothes to reveal one's true nature in its pristine purity. The essential true nature does not become soiled with the content of one's thoughts or personality. It is merely overlaid and hidden. To uncover it is the sadhu's greatest challenge.

DISPASSIONATE DETACHMENT

The state of mind and being that is considered to be the ideal for a sadhu is one of 'vairagya', which means, in short, dispassionate detachment. In Sanskrit, 'vai' denotes dry, and 'raga' refers to, variously, attachment, passion, desire and so on. So, a drying up of attachments is defined as vairagya.

The concept of vairagya is actually a lot more profound than is connoted in this somewhat one-sided literal translation of the term. It is probably the seed of vairagya in an individual that leads to him or her opting to become a sadhu. It might begin as a sort of restlessness with oneself and one's life, which might be going along fine in worldly terms. But, the individual has felt a stirring, which might develop over time into a calling. How is this different from the itch for change that anybody might feel, an urge to get out of a rut that most people feel from time to time? Not everybody who feels some kind of ennui, or a mid-life crisis, ends up a sadhu.

I think the difference might lie in the depth and extent of the feeling, and also one's own response to it. If it can be entertained away by doing something one will normally not do, like getting a tattoo or riding a motorbike, or even changing careers, then what is being experienced is not vairagya. Vairagya is a call for a complete and radical change, one that will shake the very foundations of one's being. It might begin as a restlessness, but it will not be quietened or mollycoddled into submission. It requires a specific response from the depths of the being. And this has to do with the beginning of a search of a lifetime, or many lifetimes. Though becoming a sadhu is a very specific response, it is part of the bouquet before the seeker. For, that is what one becomes once one has resolved to respond to the vairagya brooding in one's breast.

As far as I can see, sadhus are of two kinds – those who are genuine seekers, and the escapists. It is a well-known and an accepted fact that large numbers of people take to a sadhu's life in India because they are looking for an escape from something, which might be poverty, destitution, joblessness, or unpleasant

Saffron-clad women sadhus, known as sadhvis, stand in line to await their turn at a Kumbh Mela. While the nagas are allowed to charge into the Ganga for their ritual baths, others, especially women, are expected to be orderly and dignified.

Facing page: A black-clad sadhu, most probably follower of an aghora cult, stands on one leg before a funeral pyre, with his ritual skulls around him. The main practice of the aghori is to perfect his dispassionate detachment, which is aided by living and meditating in cremation grounds.

A sadhu's trident, the Sanskrit term for which is 'trishool'. It is the weapon associated with Shiva, and the sadhus who carry tridents are usually his devotees who use the trident as a tool in worship, rather than as a weapon.

Facing page: A sadhu sits before his 'dhuni', a small fire that sadhus light in front of themselves as they settle down for a period of meditation or any other spiritual practice. The dhuni was meant to keep away wild animals in forests, and also act as a signal of the sadhu's practice that should not be disturbed.

family situations, and so on. The latter is illustrated by instances of children joining bands of itinerant sadhus to escape abusive parents.

In a country like India with its socio-economic problems, and the poverty in which a large part of the population lives, it might not be too off the mark to conjecture that perhaps, the proportion of sadhus in the category of escapists is likely to be greater than those who take to sannyas because of reasons of vairagya and a need to focus on spiritual seeking to the exclusion of all else. If it is so, then sannyas becomes another 'thing' of the world, even a means for earning a kind of a livelihood. Who knows, perhaps the escapist sadhus too find something of value as they live a life of voluntary poverty, austere living, and an adherence to yogic and other spiritual disciplines?

HOLY MYTH

I have often heard sadhus being described as the 'holy men of India'. To my mind, this is at best a partial understanding of who a sadhu is. They are holy only to the extent that they are on a spiritual quest, which in many instances might play out in the context of a religion or an established spiritual tradition. Holiness in an Indian setting conjures up images of temples, priests, sacred flames being waved around deities, complex rites, colourful rituals and so on. A sadhu might have nothing to do with any of these.

This is mainly because a sadhu is outside the purview of the mainstream religion that governs much of the 'holiness' non-Indians tend to associate with the country. They are casteless, having left all such affiliations behind them along with their names which in India usually contain some indication of caste. While holy rituals have for centuries been the prerogative of caste Brahmins, who follow a strict set of instructions to maintain and enforce ritual purity, and therefore are the designated priests who are conductors of rituals and of worship, as well as rites of passage associated with birth, marriage and death.

A sadhu is not quite a part of this kind of worldly holiness, which underlies a basic need that human beings have for auspiciousness and feeling blessed. An entire body of sacred rites and rituals, designed to make holy or make auspicious, has sprung from this need. Deep down all of us know that we rarely have complete control over our lives and circumstances. Life often brings us things we might least expect at that point, and our best-laid plans can go completely awry because something quite unforeseen happens.

Holy rituals hand human beings a proverbial straw to cling to as they attempt to navigate this world of uncertainty. They form a kind of a psychological safety net – we might feel that doing this or that might protect us and our loved ones from harm, or wearing a charm or a suitable gem will ward off anything unfavourable. Or, we might want to have some way of ensuring success, that by doing something or wearing something, we will be able to script into the story of our lives an accomplishment when we need it the most. So, students preparing for crucial examinations will have mantras spoken over them, and new brides and grooms will go through a battery of rituals to make sure that the commencement of their lives together is nothing short of the most auspicious that it can be.

All very human and understandable, we might say, when we think of these factors that govern the need for holiness in human beings. Why would a sadhu not participate in these, then?

Sadhus revel in their ritual bath in the Ganga.

Facing page: A sadhu performs the headstand – sirshasana – the performance of which is thought to enhance the flow of vital energy or prana in the body.

Following pages: Smoking the chillum is common among sadhus. Here, they are seen deep in conversation at a tea shop.

This brings us back to the quality of dispassionate detachment, and its importance for a sadhu, which we touched upon in the previous section. To be dispassionate is to weigh the positive and the negative equally on the scales of life, and to view one with as much equanimity as the other, remaining unaffected by either. This dispassion is a natural outcome of the process of understanding everything as part of a whole, rather than being separate and unconnected parts.

If we are in a universe where everything is part of the divine, and everything is connected with everything else by a spark of the divine, then there is no scope for imperfection. I might perceive something as imperfect because, in that moment, it does not suit my vision of how things should be. Letting go of this 'shouldness' opens up the door to the 'isness' of life. Once we accept that this is, it simply is, and there is no other way it 'should' be, we have slipped into a dispassionate state of being.

Then, there is no need for safety nets either, no need to try and safeguard ourselves against the vagaries of life. The dispassionate sadhu is ready for whichever way the waves of life might toss him, and has thus no need for charms and rituals, either to stave off bad luck or to bring good luck. For, they are two sides of the same coin of reality to him.

An interesting understanding of this view is proffered by the branch of Tantra known as Aghora. The term 'aghora' in Sanskrit means 'that which is not dark', and is a name used for the ascetic-god, Shiva. 'Ghora' refers to darkness, and 'a-ghora' is its opposite. The followers of this form of Tantra are known as 'aghori', and worship Shiva in his Aghora aspect – he who dispels darkness.

The main practice expected of the aghori is to perfect his dispassionate detachment, at least initially all his efforts are geared towards removing the sense of self and other, this and that, seeing and behaving, as if everything is part of the one divine whole. Living and meditating in 'smashans', designated grounds for cremation, is a constant reminder of the truth of death, the movement inherent in created life. Where there is a beginning it comes intertwined with an end too.

Aghoris will test their understanding of oneness through deliberate consumption of articles considered unclean and inedible, like the raw or cooked flesh of corpses, urine, faeces and so on, which is also a direct challenge to notions of ritual purity held by the mainstream Brahmanical religion, the 'holy men', of which Aghora is a fringe offshoot. These practices are also psychological tools with which to break down the tendency of the human mind to compartmentalise reality and view it in fragments it labels 'good', 'bad', 'disgusting' or 'wholesome'. If all is part of the one, what is good and what is bad? The attempt is to break through this fragmented perspective and get to a direct experience of wholeness.

In doing so, Aghori sadhus also tap into a basic tenet of the larger Tantric philosophy – that broken down to its essentials, all matter is energy. Energy, according to the Tantric worldview, is the building block of the universe. It might exist in different forms, and in different shapes and sizes, but everything is essentially energy. It changes from one form to another and part of the Tantric's repertoire is to be able to manipulate energy from one form to another.

The attempt is to focus on the true form, the actual nature of everything, which is the same – energy. It only appears to be different, but inherently everything is the same. By this token, there is no difference between rotting flesh in a cremation ground and fragrant consecrated food (prasad) offered to the deity in a temple. Holy and unholy, thus, are myths, created by the mind to make sense of the world. Letting go of these is a task the aghori sadhu must accomplish as a requisite aspect of his sadhana.

A SEEKER'S STORY

It is believed that sadhus have been wandering this land for at least as long as civilization has existed in India, and could date back to the first known inhabitants of the subcontinent – the Indus Valley Civilization dated around the fourth century BCE – though this is a claim that might be contested, like a lot of other conjectures about that mighty and mysterious civilization. But spiritual wanderers had at least begun roaming the land in the early Vedic period (mid-second to mid-first millennium BCE), and the tradition was well-established by the time the Buddha set out from his home on his quest in the sixth century BCE. The Buddha was born Siddhartha Gautama in 563 BCE to Suddhodhana, a chieftain of the Sakya clan, and his wife, Maya. Suddhodhana's state lay at the foothills of the Himalayas, with the bustling Kapilavastu as its capital. Later Buddhist texts ascribe the status of a great and very wealthy king to Suddhodhana, which was probably not so, since the state was a republic, and Suddhodhana an elected 'raja' (ruler). Even so, Siddhartha was born into a life of comfort, with the possibility of succeeding his father if he proved to be an able administrator.

Thoughts of governance were, however, far from young Siddhartha's mind. A pensive child, he would often remain immersed in thought. This caused his father much anxiety since, according to Buddhist mythology, it was prophesied at the time of Siddhartha's birth that he was destined for greatness, but either as a 'chakravartin' (world-ruler), or a spiritual master. A spiritual life, then as now,

meant detachment from the conventions of society and worldly pursuits, and like most parents, Suddhodhana was understandably alarmed at this prospect of 'losing' his son.

The intense young Siddhartha lived in an age not unlike our own. Not only because trade and commerce flourished, but also because there was arising an attitude of questioning towards the dominant religion, Vedic Hinduism. A caste system existed, and its character as a loose organisation of professions in the Rig Vedic period, had solidified into a rigid hierarchy that dominated every aspect of life – from one's occupation, to who one could or could not marry, to the social relationships one maintained.

Caste also determined the upbringing one received, and being a Kshatriya (the ruler/warrior caste), Siddhartha was brought up accordingly. This meant emphasis on learning useful skills for administration and governance and on physical sport, than on the pursuit of knowledge. A bright mind inclined towards deep thought, Siddhartha might have found his environment intellectually unsatisfying, especially since the Brahmins took their caste-role as 'keepers of knowledge' very seriously and had monopolised scriptural and religious learning by actively excluding non-Brahmins from it.

In this milieu, being a Kshatriya meant, in a way, being spiritually less-enfranchised. Young Siddhartha probably felt this keenly, and many years later as the Buddha he would denounce the caste system, and forbid his sangha (community of seekers) from having anything to do with it. This reform might have come from the caste claustrophobia he experienced in his youth, but what seems more likely to have led the Buddha to offer equal access to the spiritual to all, is an understanding of the ultimate interconnectedness and so a oneness of all beings.

An image of Siddhartha as the Buddha, the enlightened one. He is possibly one of the best-known examples of a spiritual wanderer in the world.

Facing page: A sadhu poses before a wall mural of the Hindu monkey-god, Hanuman, who is considered an ideal devotee for his exemplary and selfless service rendered to Rama, for which he is worshipped.

In fact, the caste system and its constrictive influence on the lives of so many were only one symptom of a deeper malaise. Vedic Hinduism had degenerated into a maze of numerous, intricate rituals that only the Brahmins claimed to know the meaning of. The dominant religion, therefore, had nothing to offer to serious spiritual seekers, who abounded in the India of sixth century BCE.

This hunger for spiritual experience was happening at a time of immense prosperity. Siddhartha's society was a rich agrarian one. And it was perhaps the abundance of wealth and the consequent 'good life' that prompted many young men to delve into what lay beyond. Prosperity freed minds from survival concerns, thus enabling them to explore and evolve other aspects of their potentiality.

In this environment, with the engagement of so many bright young minds in spiritual life, a reaction to the mechanistic performance of rituals and blood sacrifices of the Vedic religion was inevitable. There started in the seventh century BCE a reform movement that began adopting new paths towards spiritual goals and examining others that had up till then, existed at the periphery of religion.

Of all these new streams of thought perhaps the most radical was that which stemmed from texts called the Upanishads. This believed all existence as being pervaded by the One, known as the Brahman, and denied the validity and worship thereof of numerous deities. Another philosophy in vogue was Samkhya which saw creation as a manifestation of two elements – purusha (consciousness) and prakriti (matter). In addition, the ancient ascetic tradition of 'paribbajakas' (literally, seekers) and 'sramanas' (strivers) was given renewed attention and their meditative practices studied with interest.

By the time Siddhartha was born, this movement had become widespread and powerful and was increasingly engaging in fierce debates and public disputations with ritualistic religion. It is possible that these voices impacted and attracted Siddhartha as a young prince in Kapilavastu.

When he was sixteen, Siddhartha was married to Yashodhara, a princess of great beauty. It is said that he lived a life of indulgence; nights of revelry flowed into days filled with all kinds of pleasures. Perfumed, oiled, clothed in the most expensive silks, Siddhartha sported and hunted, patronised musicians and made love. By material standards, ancient or modern, young Siddhartha had it all. And then...what?

By the time he was twenty-nine, the Sakya prince probably began to wonder whether this was all that there was to life. An intelligent person, he began looking around for avenues to deepen and engage his mind. Some sort of an awakening probably occurred, that brought him to the realization of the vast and as yet untapped potential that lay within him. Expected to live a nobleman's life, Siddhartha was beginning to acknowledge his own need to move beyond it. Slowly but surely, the time was approaching when Siddhartha would have no option but to deal with this inner urge.

An eleventh century AD black basalt idol that depicts the Buddha touching the earth as witness to his enlightenment – the bhumisparsha mudra.

Facing page: A priest garlands statues of deities at a Jain temple in Ranakpur, Rajasthan, dedicated to the tirthankara, Adinath.

This was also the point when Siddhartha began considering issues that he had not had the chance to give much thought to earlier. For instance, 'the Four Great Sights' that Buddhist scriptures credit with changing the course of his life—that of an old man, a sick man, a corpse and an ascetic—are perhaps meant to be symbolic of Siddhartha's thought process, rather than meant to be taken literally as actual events. It also means that he was looking around with questioning eyes and along with issues of individual fulfilment, was considering the various circumstances that characterise the human condition, like death and disease. Here we see the sowing of the seeds of compassion that was to become an important part of his teachings as the Buddha.

As Siddhartha's mind ripened in contemplation, he felt the need to move on to a life of absolute spiritual commitment. The time had come to renounce his identity as Siddhartha Gautama.

Having cut off his long hair with his sword and donning the yellow robes of an ascetic, Siddhartha probably inspected the spiritual scene for a teacher. There was plenty of choice available to him. A vibrant sramana ascetic tradition had always existed, even if on the margins of Vedic Hinduism. But constant warfare, a higher than ever degree of mass material prosperity, and the questioning of Brahmanical monopoly over religion had perhaps swelled the numbers of those opting out of society to find the truth for themselves.

Siddhartha settled upon Alara Kalama, who had 300 disciples, as his first teacher, more out of urgency to get started than anything else. He quickly mastered what Kalama had to teach – disciplining the mind to enter the 'sphere of nothingness'. Then finding that his teacher had nothing else to offer, and that what he had learnt was by itself not the realization he sought, Siddhartha left.

The meditative methods that Siddhartha learnt from his initial teachers found an echo later in his teachings as the Buddha, in the form of useful tools to help quieten the mind by leading it away from its usual engagements. However, the quietened mind is not necessarily a mind that has understood, or is fulfilled. So Siddhartha's need to move on.

A sadhu wreathed in the smoke from his chillum.

Facing page: A close-up of a sadhu's face stained with vibrant colours – turmeric yellow and vermillion on the forehead. It presents a conspicuous contrast to the ash-smeared faces and bodies of sadhus of the Shaivite lineages.

Next, he went to Uddaka Ramaputta, from whom he learnt the Upanishadic concept of the one Absolute that manifests in everything. He also learnt to enter the meditative state that is neither consciousness nor unconsciousness. Yet, this too, was not the fulfilment he sought. Siddhartha left again, and having had enough of teachers began a rigorous ascetic practice on his own, in the company of five others.

Even though Siddhartha had gracefully moved on after learning whatever he could from his teachers, he continued with conventional ascetic practice. Why? Probably because that was the model available to him and until he reached the ultimate understanding, which could not but be his own, he had to make do with what he had.

For the next six years, Siddhartha remained immersed in deep concentration. It was a harsh, merciless practice. To subjugate his body, he would eat next to nothing, at times restricting himself to one grain of rice a day. Meditating in the forests near the city of Uruvela (in the present-day state of Bihar, south-east India), he denied himself protection against the scorching summers and the harsh winters. Soon, he was more dead than alive.

A second century AD black stone sculpture from Gandhara, West Pakistan, depicts Siddhartha in this state brought on by self-flagellatory penance, his body wasted away, each detail of skeleton visible under a skin that was no more than

a thin film stretched over bones. In the Pali text, Majjhima Nikaya, the Buddha recounts, 'My body reached a state of extreme emaciation. My limbs became like the dry and knotted joints of bamboo...If I wanted to touch my belly-skin, I encountered my backbone...If I rubbed my limbs, the hair, rotted at the roots, came away in my hands.'

And at the end of it all, he still hadn't reached the fulfilment he sought.

Six years into this asceticism, and Siddhartha knew he was doing something wrong. He was no closer to realization than he had been at the beginning of the practice. With the question, 'Might there not be another way to awakening?' echoing in his mind, Siddhartha ended his severe penance by accepting a bowl of rice from Sujata, a young woman. The story is delightful because of the feminine intervention — that and the food are a sign of Siddhartha's veering away from ascetic extremes, towards a less harsh middle path in his practice.

Even as his companions of six years set their faces against him, disgusted at what seemed to them a giving up of asceticism, a revived Siddhartha probably washed in the Nilanjana river, and sat under a nearby bodhi (Ficus Indica) tree.

Till now, Siddhartha had been striving for realization, he had been exerting his will. Now, he remembered, from a time in his childhood, an effortless flowing into perfect equanimity. Taking that as his lodestone, Siddhartha felt an ease envelop him. The tightness in his body and mind softened.

A mural depicts a scene from the Buddha's life, who is easily recognisable by the halo around his head and his physical prominence in the depiction. He is surrounded by his bhikkhus, who came from all walks of life and formed an inclusive, egalitarian community in defiance of the caste rules and spiritual dominance claimed by the Brahmins of the time.

Six days later, over the four watches of night, it is said that Siddhartha realized his true nature, and that of Reality. Although the actual nature of what happened is mysterious, we do know that there was a sense of conclusion, and of a supreme connection. This he expressed through a simple gesture—that of touching the earth—when asked for proof of his enlightenment. That simple gesture conveyed that through his awakening, the Buddha had realized his connection with everything everywhere.

Siddhartha, prince of the Sakyas, had ceased to exist, as had the student, and the ascetic. From under the Bodhi tree, rose one who had awakened to his true, enlightened nature.

The Buddha Sakyamuni, sage of the Sakyas.

The story of Siddhartha's transformation to the Buddha is a powerful one, as it outlines the beginning of his ascetic journey as a sadhu, in a milieu where

spiritual seeking was gaining momentum and becoming a path of choice for those dissatisfied with mainstream religion as well as a materialistically oriented life. Learning from his own experience the importance of living a sadhu's life for spiritual realization, the Buddha founded his order, a sangha of renunciates.

He, along with his contemporary, the Jain teacher Mahavira, was one of the first to organise the sadhu's free-spirited wandering and give it a definitive shape and structure. It was also the beginning of sadhus' orders that channelized spiritual aspiration quite decisively towards a particular goal, that of enlightenment. Simultaneously, they lent legitimacy to a life-choice that up until then had been outside the pale of society. For a while, their growing popularity made the sadhu's life a preferred alternative for many, from all walks of life, as is evident from historical sources that describe vibrant and diverse communities as springing up around the Buddha and Mahavira.

SECTS AND SANGHAS

The Middle Path

A sadhu serves other sadhus during a community meal at a dharamshala (a charitable guesthouse), during the Kumbh Mela.

Facing page: A sadhu outfitted rather dramatically in ash, rows of rudraksha beads and marigold garlands, poses for the camera at his akhara's camp during a Kumbh Mela.

The organisation of hitherto free-floating sramanas into structured communities with sets of laws and codes of conduct was part of the spiritual ferment that gripped India in the sixth and fifth centuries BCE. There was a growing disenchantment with the mainstream Vedic religion, which increasingly had become entangled in the complexities of propitiatory rites and rituals, and offered little recourse to one who sought a direct connection with truth.

People who were sensitive to this need were checking out of the conventional householder's life, and hitting the road in a bid to find teachers or tools that might help them delve deeper into the nature of the self and of life. Siddhartha Gautama, as we saw in the previous chapter, was one such young man. Vardhaman Mahavira was another.

There are stunning similarities between the lives of the two great sramanas, which can inspire the conjecture that though they were extraordinary individuals, their lives were also indicative of the circumstances of their times. Vardhaman, too, was a prince born, to powerful parents, King Siddaratha and his wife, Trishala, close to the present-day city of Patna in the Indian state of Bihar.

Like Siddhartha, Vardhaman, too, led the privileged life of a future ruler until the age of thirty, when existential ennui made him leave home and take to the life of a wandering sramana. He practised intensely all the time and lived a severely austere life, giving up everything, even his clothes, and barely eating enough to survive. After twelve years, his practice fruitioned, and he achieved enlightenment.

The reason he came to be known as 'Mahavira', which means 'great hero', is because he attained enlightenment through his own efforts, which were understood to be nothing short of heroic. It is interesting to note that at this time, true heroism had come to be equated with the spiritual journey, and it was being felt that to conquer one's own fears and negative psychology and habit patterns was a far greater achievement than conquering lands and peoples.

अग्रवाल किराना स्टोर्स
इलाहाबाद

Idols depicting Jain 'tirthankaras'. Literally 'bridge-makers', tirthankaras are believed to rescue human beings enmeshed in the suffering of samsara using the raft of knowledge. Vardhaman Mahavira is thought to be the twenty-fourth, and last, tirthankara of the present age.

This is indicative of the mood of the times too, where more and more people were resorting to spiritual seeking, and it had come to have pre-eminence as a standard of human accomplishment. If one excelled in the battlefield, and subdued an enemy, one could at best be a vira, a hero. To be a maha vira, a great hero, one needed to do something that required far greater courage – the subjugation of the ego-self, and the realization of one's true nature.

ORGANISED ORDERS

Though their philosophies differed on significant counts, some of the Buddha and Mahavira resonated with one another and were a reflection of the kind of change they attempted to bring not only in the understanding of spirituality, and the path of the sramana, but in the socio-economic-political sphere as well. These mainly had to do with an emphasis on non-violence, a movement away from the caste system, and a stress on the spiritual equality, and ability, of all human beings regardless of caste and gender.

These were direct reactions to the caste-ridden Vedic religion where the Brahmins, the caste of priests and learned men, had appropriated the entire sphere of sacredness, and would dole out rituals and rites to all other castes for a fee. The lowest castes had no access to this sphere at all. Their tenet on non-violence had to do with the use of animal sacrifice in the Vedic religion as a way

Like Jain tirthankaras, Mahayana Buddhism (whose one version, Vajrayana, is practised in Tibet) has bodhisattvas who in their infinite compassion offer the teachings of 'dharma' to help beings cross the misery of samsara.

of propitiating the gods, which had over time become excessive and was deemed unnecessary and even heinous by the Buddha and Mahavira, who also emphasised on vegetarianism.

It is useful to look at both these extraordinary spiritual teachers in the context of their time and age, and the circumstances that existed during that period. Though the spiritual tools they devised to help the seeker's inner growth might have been unique and original, they were also rooted in practices of their times, one of which seems to have been the organisation of sramanas into communities.

Both Mahavira and the Buddha founded monastic orders that have endured till the twenty-first century – in India and elsewhere. That this was pretty much a feature of the times is evident from this quote from the Mahaparinibbana Sutra, which mentions, '...those ascetics, samana and Brahmins who have orders and followings, who are teachers, well-known and famous as founders of schools, and popularly regarded as saints, like Purana Kassapa, Makkhali Gosala, Ajita Kesakambali, Pakudha Kaccayana, Sanjaya Belatthaputta, and the Nigantha Nataputta.' Both Buddhist and Jain literature of the time mentions most of these teachers as ones who had formed communities of sramanas under their guidance.

The Buddhist 'sangha', or community of seekers, began with the Buddha's first, post-enlightenment sermon at Sarnath, where he accepted his five former ascetic companions as his followers. For the next 49 years until his death, the

A group of monks pose for a group photograph at the Talok monastery in Tibet, famous for its wood carvings. The Sangha or community of seekers is one of the three jewels of Buddhism, the other two being the Buddha and the Dharma.

Facing page: Young Tibetan monks practise the traditional form of debate in a monastery's courtyard. Debating the finer points of philosophy is an essential aspect of the training in logic that is imparted in the various schools of Tibetan Vajrayana Buddhism.

Buddha roamed the country, walking through cities and villages, stopping often to discourse and converse. Wherever he went, many men, and later women too, accepted his teachings, some as lay followers, others as bhikkhus and bhikkhunis (monks and nuns).

In the beginning, there appeared to have been no formal initiation into the sangha. The aspirant's commitment and the Buddha's assent, non-verbal at times, were thought sufficient. As was customary among ascetics of the time, the bhikkhu would then shave his head as a symbol of his renunciation and simply follow the Buddha, in his journeys and in his teachings.

As the sangha grew rapidly, the Buddha encouraged his monks to ordain, thereby enabling the sangha to grow organically and develop a life of its own. He did outline an elementary ceremony though, in which the initiate was to seek refuge in the three 'jewels': Buddha, dhamma and sangha by repeating thrice:

Buddham sharanam gacchhami
Dhammam sharanam gacchhami
Sangham sharanam gacchhami
I take refuge in the Buddha
I take refuge in the Dhamma (Pali for 'dharma')
I take refuge in the Sangha.

That this ritual-like ceremony was not really necessary for spiritual engagement might have occurred to the Buddha, given his own possible experience as a Kshatriya nobleman of Brahmanical rituals, where the means had become ends in

themselves and tended to lead away from the metaphysical core. Yet, he perhaps was also aware of man's basic need to lend a framework to his actions, which is what a ritual does. And a new monk probably needed the reassurance. Apart from this concession, primary Buddhism seems to have had no ritual.

Initially, when the sangha was still more like a band of followers, the Buddha would journey with them all the year round, except during the monsoons when torrential rains forced them to seek shelter in caves and later, in 'viharas' (retreats). For a few months every year, wandering came to a halt. It is likely that this time was used for introspection.

With the expansion of the sangha and the building of monasteries by wealthy patrons and kings, some monks appear to have been allowed to live settled lives. These settlements were usually right at the periphery of towns, and not far away into forests, as was customary among renunciates. One reason might have been that the Buddha did not wish for his sangha to exist in isolation. Rather, he envisaged a social duty for his bhikkhus.

A Buddhist bhikkhu is not a 'monk' in a Christian, or even an Indian sramana sense. The Buddha probably saw him as a 'sharesman' – one who received a

A Jain sadhu sits at the feet of the giant statue of Bahubali at Shravanabelagola in the south Indian state of Karnataka. The frail pilgrim presents a striking contrast to the feet of the idol, which is fifty-seven feet tall.

share. His begging for alms was symbolic of his renunciation of possessions and therefore of his reliance on common wealth. In that sense, the bhikkhu was very much a part of society and often had a symbiotic relationship with patron householders, with whom he shared his 'dhamma' (knowledge) and offered a spiritual perspective on worldly matters.

This integration of sangha and society appears to have been a first in India where, for as long as anybody could remember, spiritual seekers had wandered out of society. The Buddha led them right back in, thereby giving the sangha an integral vision that was really another articulation of the middle path, which took into account both social responsibility and spiritual seeking.

Rulers who embraced the Buddha's dhamma, like the powerful Bimbisara of Magadha and Pasenadi of Kosala, among others, granted his sangha amnesty from the laws of their lands. Thus it fell upon the Buddha to ensure that all members of his sangha behaved appropriately and that the kings' exemption was not misused. For, we must remember, that the vast sangha included people from all castes and social classes who were not used to living in such close proximity with one another. Even though they were following the Buddha's teachings, it is possible

A group of Jain sadhvis in prayer. Though Jain philosophy is avowedly atheistic, there exists belief in the benedictory powers of gods and goddesses who preside over the natural and human realms. The jinas, the enlightened ones, are also prayed to for guidance and inspiration.

Facing page: A solitary 'Jain' pilgrim. Due to their strong belief in ahimsa, non-violence, Jain monastics avoid motorised vehicles whose use might result in the loss of life of insects on the road, and prefer to walk even over long distances.

that tensions arose and the scriptures do record instances where quarrels had broken out among monks even during the Buddha's lifetime.

It is interesting to note that the Buddha seems to have regulated the sangha along the lines of a republic. Perhaps an echo of the years he spent in the Sakyan republic? In the sangha republic, the Buddha's position was equivalent to that of a ruler by virtue of being the founder. Next to him were his chief disciples Sariputta and Moggallana, who owed their position to spiritual merit. In due course, a leadership group developed in the sangha composing of monks senior in ordination and those who were said to have attained 'arahantship' (status of arahant, conqueror of afflictive emotions). Important decisions were taken by the entire assembly where, it appears that, any monk or novitiate could voice his opinion. There was however no vote and the matter was discussed until everybody reached a consensus, indicated by silence.

Apart from basic sangha rules pertaining to non-violence, non-possession, celibacy, and eating before noon, most others were subject to change. The greatly detailed dos and don'ts, especially for women, that we now see in Buddhism were probably codified well after the Buddha. For during his lifetime, he appears to have always searched for the middle path in this matter, as in all others. For instance, once disturbed in the middle of a discourse by blessings when he

Detail of a painting from Orissa that depicts Lord Jagannath. The image echoes the famed idol in the Jagannath Temple in Puri, which is the site of a beloved annual festival when, in an elaborate chariot, the deity leaves the temple and mingles with devotees.

Facing page: An elderly sadhu picks up a load of bricks with his penis. A lifetime devoted to yogic practices is supposed to enhance the flow of prana in one's body, and endow it with extraordinary physical, mental and spiritual strength.

sneezed, the Buddha forbade such blessings or any response to them. Learning however, that this was being considered rude by townspeople, he allowed the practice. This example, although seemingly trifle,, illustrates the openness of mind that the Buddha brought to everything.

PRACTICAL APPROACH

The sramana orders, which could be considered to be the originators of the sadhus of today, differed significantly from the mainstream Brahmanical Vedic religion of their day. As mentioned before, the Buddhist and Jain sramanas were part of this parallel stream that developed, gained in strength, and dominated the spiritual landscape of the Indian subcontinent, until the Hindu revival initiated by Adi Shankaracharya in the eighth and ninth centuries CE.

As outlined earlier in the chapter, the different sramana movements had some common points. A major one was the emphasis on direct experience and practice, which is also borne out by the very meaning of the term sramana, which is 'one who makes an effort'. This effort lies at the heart of the sramana philosophy, if one could imagine one such integrated body of thoughts and ideas collected from among the many that existed together in the same field and at the same time.

The result of this reliance on self-effort was that the sramanas did not feel

compelled to propitiate gods created out of natural phenomena, like the Vedic religion. The early Aryans were nomadic cattle-herders and consequently their gods had to do with invoking beneficent natural circumstances for their flocks to thrive. Often referred to as the 'male sky gods', these deities wielded enormous clout over the Aryan psyche, as is indicated in the hymns of the Rig Veda.

The sramanas did not believe in creator deities. Jain philosophy is avowedly atheistic, while the Buddha was famously silent on the question of God. The sramanas wished to prioritize self-effort over all else, which is why they discouraged dependence on external agencies and powers. They put the onus of bettering one's life, of growth and development, or of negativity and suffering, on the individual. If there was suffering, it was because of the mental patterns, the desires and frustrations, of the individual. Ignorance of the cause of suffering was why, quite simply, human being suffered.

Rooting out this ignorance was in the hands of each individual, who could do it by practices such as watching the mind, becoming conscious of the different levels of one's being and gradually the core. The disciplines of yoga, designed to bring the individual body, mind, spirit in alignment and union with cosmic

A group of sadhus engaged in conducting rituals possibly pertaining to their individual practice.

Facing page: A practitioner of Tantra poses with his skull, which plays a central role in Tantric rituals.

Sadhus light up their collective chillum, while one holds it in his hand the other applies the matchstick.

Facing page: A sadhu stands on one leg, his trident before him. His right hand, raised in a gesture of benediction, echoes that of the goddess in the large painting behind him.

consciousness, and other practicable philosophies that developed as a result of this endeavour, took power away from the male sky gods and handed it back to the individual. If one could access a deeper consciousness through meditative practice, and truly understand the nature of mind and spirit, one had no need to invoke or placate the wind or the sun or the rain. Thus, the sramanas had little use for the services of the Brahmin priest or his repertory of Vedic invocations.

The other, rather significant way in which the sramanas placed the individual at the centre of his or her own universe was through the doctrine of karma. In common parlance, karma means action. Philosophically, it is much more than that. The seed of an action begins with a thought and an intention. That is where karma is located, and where the long cycle of its fruition begins. The doctrine has several interpretations made by schools of thought and teachers through the centuries. The more conventional one is that once the seed of a karma has been planted in the universe, it will fruition over time, which could be anytime in this lifetime, or in another one, or yet another one.

The doctrine of karma is the principal fuel for the belief in the transmigration of souls. Individual karma, created by thought, intention, feeling or deed, are sowed like seeds by human beings in almost every moment of their lives, especially if they are not mindful of it, like most of us. These seeds germinate and mature, and await the correct combination of circumstances to express themselves in the life of that human being. It is believed that since all the karma we make in a lifetime cannot possibly be exhausted in it, a component of the self, moves into a new lifetime with the karmic information embedded into it.

This to me sounds a lot like genetic information that lies coded in DNA being passed on from one generation to the next. Only, the karmic information has the potential of being exhausted. Which could either be through a natural process of culmination that would take several lifetimes and is potentially never-ending, because we keep making new karma all the time, or, it can be a conscious, speeded up process, put into motion by the 'jnani', the knower of truth.

Because samsara, this created world, ensures suffering, the goal of the spiritual journey according to the sramanas is to cycle out of it by shrugging off the yoke of karma that ties the individual down to infinite successive rebirths. This can only occur if one is consciously exhausting the stack of pre-existing karma, along with taking care not to make any new one, achieving the state of moksha (release) or nirvana (exhaustion). This became the avowed goal of sramanic practices, and different systems advocated different ways of going about this, through conscious, non-harming living, or the yogic disciplines to tame body and mind, or through ways of wearing down the ego that was held responsible for creating new karma.

It is interesting to note that the doctrine of karma was later incorporated into mainstream religion, which was also changing through contact with the sramanas. In fact, there was a veering away from an excess of blood sacrifices and ritualism because of the groundswell against some of these things, caused by the stand taken by the sramana movements. Mainstream religion ceased to be the monolith it once was, and began accepting into itself some changes including the adoption of the sramanic understanding of karma, which later was to become fairly central to its worldview, in particular as espoused by the non-dual philosophy of Advaita Vedanta.

HINDU RENAISSANCE

There began a decline in Buddhism, and a simultaneous renaissance in the Hindu traditions from the eighth century CE onwards. This renaissance was in part powered by an assimilation of practices and philosophies of the sramanic movements, and in part by the appearance of philosophers like Adi Sankaracharya, who through his propagation of Advaita Vedanta, helped the Hindu traditions to move quite decisively towards a philosophy that was decidedly different from the ritualistic religion that had existed before.

Advaita Vedanta spoke of a unitive view of reality, known as Brahman, as opposed to the polytheistic one advocated in the Vedas. Though a multiplicity of divinity remained in popular culture and actually exists till today, the diverse deities were explained as aspects of the One, parts of the same divine oneness. They came to be incorporated into the overarching and all-encompassing context of Brahman, and the doctrine of karma and its attendant theory of transmigration of souls, also came to be part of the Vedantic worldview.

The level of reality that we engage in every day, and which we navigate through our senses, came to be explained as maya, the veil of illusion that keeps us from knowing reality as it is – one, not dual. Duality is enforced upon us by the senses

that make us experience our own self and personality as one, and the rest of the world as 'the other'. To cut through this duality of perspective came to be regarded as the goal of the Vedantin, followed by a direct perception of the divine oneness of the cosmos.

One of the effects of Buddhism on revived Hinduism was the establishment of a monastic order by Adi Sankaracharya, which he is thought to have modelled on the Buddhist monastic sangha. This was the beginning of formalised monasticism within the purview of the organised Hindu religion, which was further established through four mathas or monastic centres, which continue till today. Located in the four extremities of the Indian subcontinent, these centres also served the purpose of binding a diverse land with a universal creed, which their case was Advaita Vedanta.

These four mathas were at Jyotirmath in Uttarakhand (north), Sringeri in Karnataka (south), Dwaraka in Gujarat (west), and Puri in Orissa (east). Adi Sankaracharya designated each of the four mathas as a keeper of one of the four Veda, with the responsibility of researching and continuing the teachings and traditions associated with them. So, Puri was given the Rig Veda, Sringeri the Yajur Veda, Dwaraka the Sama Veda, and Jyotirmath the Atharva Veda.

The heads of these mathas continue to bear the title, Sankaracharya, after their founder, who is referred to as 'Adi Sankaracharya' to denote the fact that he came first, the Sanskrit term 'adi' standing for original. The Sankaracharya of each matha nominates his successor in his lifetime, having identified the suitable candidate from among the sannyasis under his tutelage. Even so, there is no foolproof way of ensuring succession, and the seats at mathas have often remained vacant in the absence of an appropriate successor, the longest such period being at Jyotirmath, where it was without a resident Sankaracharya for 165 years at a stretch at one point. When a situation of conflicting nominees for the post arises, Sankaracharyas of other mathas are consulted and the issue resolved with their common assent.

The heads of the four mathas are always monks, having ordained as sannyasis either as very young people, or later in life after having spent some years as householders. The Sringeri Sankaracharyas are usually of the former kind, and so assume their responsibilities at a younger age, as compared to other lineages where they might be older when they come into sannyas. This is why the list of Sankaracharyas at Sringeri is much shorter than elsewhere.

The monastic tradition of Advaita Vedanta founded by Adi Sankaracharya was termed the Dasanami Sampradaya, literally, community of ten names. This title was derived by the act of bringing together ten different sects and uniting them under the tutelage of the four mathas mentioned above. The motivation was to unite all the Advaita Vedanta sects under a common umbrella, and perhaps also to offer an alternative to the monastic systems of Buddhism and Jainism to those desirous of leading a full-time contemplative life. An organised sect also made it easier for householders to support sadhus than if they were itinerant wanderers – a model of upkeep of monastics borrowed from Buddhism.

The Dasanami sadhus are known as 'ekadandi' or one stick, which is what they carry, as opposed to 'tridandi', or the three-stick-sadhus, who are adherents of Vaishnava philosophy that regards Vishnu as the supreme being. The single stick is a symbol of the central Advaita belief in the oneness principle, denoted

by Brahman, who is The One. The ekadandi sadhus are essentially Vedantin, and though they were brought together by Adi Sankaracharya, several of these sects continue to function as independent orders of monastics.

Those who ordain in the Dasanami tradition receive one of the ten names associated with it as suffixes to their sannyas names. These indicate an affiliation with one of the four mathas – 'Saraswati', 'Bharati' and 'Puri' with the

Sadhus camping under a makeshift shelter. The sadhu's lifestyle is a lesson in the impermanence of materiality – only when one realises this can one truly embark upon the quest for truth.

An ash-smeared sadhu, bedecked in an interesting floral headgear and garlands of marigold, makes for an arresting photograph.

Facing page: Passers-by make way for naga sadhus, one of whom is raising a religious slogan, even as one of the onlookers greets him with folded hands.

Sringeri matha, 'Tirtha' and 'Ashrama' with the Dwaraka matha, 'Giri', 'Parvata' and 'Sagara' with Joshimath, and 'Vana' and 'Aranya' with the Puri matha. It is to be noted that these names also signal a banding together of sadhus of that particular name into an order, and at times these orders might only be nominally affiliated with the four mathas.

One of the reasons is that the mathas tend to strictly follow caste distinctions, while the sannyas orders are more democratic and inclusive when it comes to accepting adherents. The sannyasis also don't have to live in the matha their lineage is connected to, and in fact are expected to keep up the wandering sramana's life, not stopping anywhere for too long except during the monsoons. This is another echo of the Buddha's sangha, where the monastics also roamed through the land for much of the year and stayed in one place only during the monsoons, known as the vessa retreat.

AKHARA ORGANISATION

Since the time of Adi Sankaracharya, there have occurred several changes in Hindu monasticism with the arising of new sects and communities, the effects of fresh interpretations of doctrines, and changing socio-economic circumstances in each age. What is interesting to note is that despite such changes, not just in Hindu but all monastic traditions, there have been in each era at least a few people who have displayed an affinity towards vairagya, and a movement away from the established convention towards a life of the spirit.

In north India, the different sects of the Dasanami orders became organised

over time into various 'akharas', camps of sadhus. Akhara is a term that comes from wrestling terminology, and refers to a patch of mud on which practitioners of the Indian style of wrestling learn and practise their moves. The three major akharas of sadhus that exist today are Juna, Niranjani and Mahanirvani, and they have three minor akharas affiliated to them – Avahan and Agni with Juna, Atal with Mahanirvani, and Anand with Niranjani. Of these, Juna Akhara is said to be the biggest in terms of the numbers of sadhus in its fold.

Apart from these, akharas are also categorised according to their worship of a principal deity, which usually has to do with one of those from the trinity – Brahma, Vishnu, Shiva – the creator, preserver and destroyer respectively. While the Vedantin sadhus do not believe in the supremacy of any one deity, advocating a formless truth instead in the form of Brahman, there are other streams that are oriented towards worship of a cosmic being, in form and in the persona of either of the three main deities. The Vaishnava akharas worship Vishnu as their main deity, and are also known as Vairagi akharas. The Shaiva akharas worship Shiva, while the Kalpawasis have Brahma as their prime deity.

A Tantric practitioner's hand rests on top of his ritual skull.

Rather than being loosely held bands of itinerant monks, over the centuries akharas have evolved a precise and hierarchical method of organisation and functioning. While the head of the akhara is the Mahamandaleshwar, an akhara is administered by a committee of five senior members who are elected to it during every Kumbha Mela,. The akhara is divided into eight divisions and fifty-two centres that are called 'marhi', each one of which is under the leadership of an official known as a mahant.

The phenomenon of the naga sadhu is a seemingly esoteric feature in the akhara system of monastic organisation. The nagas, usually naked, dreadlocked, their bodies smeared with the ash from funeral pyres are believed to practise the severest physical austerities and make a public appearance only during the Kumbh and Mahakumbh Melas in Hardwar, on the banks of the sacred river Ganga. The naga sadhus have a martial past and till today, in addition to their yogic disciplines, might train in the use of weapons and the martial arts.

The naga sadhus come out in full force at the Kumbh Melas, which are the largest gatherings of sadhus and lay people of faith in the country. The Sanskrit word 'kumbh' means pot, and is the sign for Aquarius in Indian astrology, under which the fair is celebrated. The Kumbh Melas follow a twelve-year cycle, with the regular Kumbh Mela held every three years, the 'Ardh Kumbh' (half Kumbh) every six years at Hardwar and Prayag (the sacred confluence of the Ganga, Yamuna and the Saraswati rivers, the last of which was mentioned in the Rig Veda but disappeared soon after), and the 'Purna Kumbh' (complete Kumbh) or the complete Kumbh is held every twelve years at four locations – Hardwar, Prayag, Ujjain and Nashik. The Mahakumbh, the great Kumbh Mela, takes place at Prayag after every twelve Purna Kumbh Melas, and thus follows a cycle of 144 years. The last Mahakumbh Mela was in 2001 and was attended by some sixty million people, making it the largest gathering of human beings ever recorded on the planet.

Where the regular Kumbh Melas are organised depends on the positioning of stars. The locations are determined through astrology, and alternate between Nashik in Maharashtra, Hardwar in the Himalayas, Prayag in Uttar Pradesh, and Ujjain in Madhya Pradesh in central India. These are all locations of ancient sacredness along the route of the great river goddess Ganga, as she makes her

way from the pristine heights of the Himalayas where she originates, to the Bay of Bengal where she unites with the ocean.

Kumbh Melas have been held since antiquity, perhaps the Vedic times. The first time they appear in written history is in the Chinese traveller Huan Tsang's accounts from the seventh century AD. It is apparent they had been going on much before that and were even then some centuries old. The sacredness associated with the Ganga does date back to the Vedic age, and it is quite plausible that the Melas came to be organised then as a way of celebrating this belief.

The myth associated with the Kumbh Melas connects them with the mythological event of the churning of the primordial ocean, undertaken by gods and demons together. The opposing forces joined hands to have the ocean yield its treasures by churning it, and placed a mountain at the centre, encircled by Vasuki, the king of the serpents. The gods held the serpent's tail and the demons his head, in order to churn the ocean. Because they had agreed to share all spoils equally the gods were in a quandary when the ocean yielded its most precious treasure – the nectar of immortality.

Fakirs pierce their cheeks with metal rods at the shrine of the Sufi saint, Khwaja Moinuddin Chishti, in Ajmer in Rajasthan. That they can do what would be physically impossible or extremely painful for most, is a proof of their faith and of the benediction of the saint.

A morning boat ride in the Holy Ganges. It joins the Yamuna at the Triveni Sangam at Allahabad, a holy confluence in Hinduism.

Sadhus being rowed in a boat on the Ganga. One of them is seen leaning back, in joyful abandon, his hands trailing in the holy waters in an almost childlike enjoyment of the moment.

Afraid that if the nectar was consumed by the demons they would become all-powerful and also immortal, the gods petitioned Vishnu, the preserver, for a way out. Vishnu sent his emissary, the bird Garuda, to steal the pot of nectar. As Garuda flew away with the pot in his beak, drops of the nectar fell at four spots along the Ganga – at Hardwar, Nashik, Ujjain and Prayag – the places where the Kumbh Melas came to be held.

All individuals who believe in the Hindu worldview try and attend the Kumbh Melas. It is especially an occasion for the akharas to come out in full force. They camp on the banks of the Ganga for the entire duration of the fair, conducting akhara business like elections of governing bodies, meeting devotees, dispensing spiritual advice, and at times, smoking chillums filled with hashish. Curious onlookers are drawn to the sight of dreadlocked, ash-smeared sadhus practising austerities like perpetually holding one hand up in the air, standing on one leg, and contorting their supple bodies into seemingly impossible yogic asanas.

The main ritual at the Kumbh Melas is the bath in the Ganga, which is considered auspicious even in normal circumstances. During the Kumbh, it becomes even more so, especially on days that are identified by astrologers as increasing the merit gained by the observance manifold. On these days, a 'shahi snan'(royal bath), is announced and rules laid out for its smooth organisation. The akharas and their sadhus are given precedence over the laity, and are given

an order in which to approach the embankment for the bath. This is at times disputed among the different akharas, with the ones given later slots feeling belittled and attempting to have them changed.

Clashes among different akharas are not unheard of and in fact were the norm in earlier times. The procession of each akhara comes in great style, accompanied by their naga sadhus that charge into the river ahead of everyone else. The heads of akharas, Mahamandaleshwars and other respected sadhus are carried on palanquins or bestride caparisoned elephants and horses.

OUTSIDE CONVENTION

It must be mentioned here that there might be an overlap between the akharas and the Dasanami system of classification of sadhus, and there are sometimes no neat divisions apparent to one who is an outsider to the at times complex world of Indian monastics. There might be yet other orders of sadhus that would be beyond the area of influence of both, like the influential Nath yogis.

Outside of the matha-akhara system there were still sramanic streams that did not become incorporated into the consolidated sadhu systems. One such was the order of the Nath yogis who trace their origin to a great yogi, Matsyendranath in the eighth and ninth centuries AD, and subsequently to his disciple, Gorakhnath. Knowledge was transmitted among the Nath yogis directly from guru to disciple, rather than read from scriptures. Disciples were, and are, initiated by a guru, who is a lineage holder in any one of the several streams that came to develop among the Nath yogis.

The Nath yogis abjured recording their teachings and spiritual practices in any form, emphasising the route of direct transmission, because it was felt that teaching is not just words the guru speaks and the disciple hears. The guru was also believed to literally transmit some of his quality of consciousness to the disciple through a mysterious process known as 'shaktipat', a term that means the fall of energy. This transmission can be effected through a look, a touch, a word, a mantra, and is believed to be an act of grace on the part of the guru towards the disciple.

The Nath yogis, unlike the matha system, live outside society and do not subsist on it, and are ungoverned by its conventions. In this sense, they are free. But not free to do as they please, rather, they are bound to follow the conventions of another kind, which are designed to bring to them the greatest freedom, that of enlightenment.

It is believed that the Nath yogis were the originators of 'sandhya bhasha' what is known as twilight language, a codified language that cannot be understood by one initiated into it by a guru. So, even when the Nath yogis wrote down the knowledge of their tradition it could not be understood by anyone outside their circle. The convention of using twilight language to veil secret and esoteric teachings and practices from the eyes of outsiders was adopted by various Tantric sects as well, for similar reasons.

In the medieval period, with the advent of Islam in India in the twelfth century, the flavour of religion in the subcontinent changed. A new spirituality developed too, with the ranks of sadhus being swelled by Sufi fakirs, many of whom also lived the life of an itinerant wanderer and practised disciplines that brought them closer to a union with God, which was also an avowed aim of the sadhus of India, though the understanding of God in different traditions was obviously different.

Though Sufism was not born in India, it acquired a distinct characteristic here, which according to some could be traced to the influence and commingling of Indian bhakti (devotion) traditions, as well as the adoption of yogic practices. These influences the Sufis made their own. Their centres and mazaars (tombs) became crucibles for the growth of a new kind of culture, one that combined a host of influences ranging from the Persian and Arabic, to the ones that had been distilled in the heat and dust of the Indian subcontinent over millennia. A new language was also born out of this commingling – Urdu – as were ways of dressing, cooking, music, dance, among many other things.

Sufism could be seen as the mystical aspect of Islam, with a central goal being to create a state of 'fitra' in one's being, described as a return to one's primordial nature. This state is a pre-requisite to discarding the dualistic perspective that sees the self as separate from the Divine. The Sufi lives simply, and must simultaneously discard negative traits in his or her character, and adopt positive traits. If this sounds like what the various Hindu and Buddhist yogis and adepts were also trying to do, it only illustrates the essential similarity of the goal of spiritual seeking.

The Sufis also came to be organised in orders, and though all adherents were required to live a life of simplicity and piety, they were not required to live as fakirs, and there was no monkhood or sannyas in the sense that there was among the Hindu, Buddhist, Jain and other sramana streams. To become a fakir was an entirely voluntary act, and the individual would make the choice, or be drawn to

it 'choicelessly'. The Sufi orders in India were – Shadhilliya, Chishti, Shattariya, Suhrawardi, Qadiri and Naqshbandi.

The baul minstrels of Bengal originated in the fifteenth century AD and symbolised a syncretism that brought together different wisdom traditions. Some believe that elements of Sufism, Vaishnava Hinduism, Tantra and Buddhism can be identified in the baul tradition. The word baul denotes one who is mad, and therefore outside the conventions of society. bauls are in essence seekers of truth, as much as sadhus, yogis and fakirs.

Music and singing are central to the baul way of life, and is also the way they connect with society. Itinerant bauls have become integral to the life of rural Bengal, where they would roam from one place to another singing songs of cosmic love that recognised the divine in everything, and at times, songs of protest and equality. Bauls wear a distinctive garment, and are often distinguishable by their one-stringed instrument, the ektara. Unlike all other sadhu traditions and orders, the bauls practise gender equality, with women being given as much an opportunity to hone their spiritual lives as the men.

A group of Baul minstrels. Music and singing are central to the Baul way of life, and is also the way they connect with society. Unlike other sadhu traditions, bauls practise gender equality, with women being given as much an opportunity to hone their spiritual lives as the men.

Kumbh and Mahakumbh Melas

The Kumbh Melas and their larger versions, the Mahakumbh Melas, are thought to be the largest religious gatherings in the world. The last Mahakumbh Mela, celebrated in 2010, reportedly saw an estimated attendance of forty million pilgrims over four months, from mid-January to mid-April, with ten million bathing in the Ganga on a single auspicious day on 14 April.

The Kumbh and Mahakumbh Melas follow a cycle of sacredness that might have begun in the Vedic period, which is tentatively dated between 1500 to 500 BC. The first historical account of these melas, however, only appears in the 7th century AD in the chronicles of the Chinese traveller, Huan Tsang.

Whenever they might have begun, the Kumbh and Mahakumbh Melas have been crucial landmark events in the Indian subcontinent, of the interplay of faith and sacredness, of belief and that which is believed in, so to speak. In this sense, they offer an invaluable insight into the spiritual psyche of this ancient land. To know how the drama of faith and belief unfolds in the mind of India, one just has to visit one of the melas, preferably the grand one that comes around every twelve years.

Pilgrims from all over the country, and now from abroad as well, arrive on the banks of the Ganga to bathe in its purifying waters. Certain days, determined by the lunar calendar, are considered more auspicious than others for the ritual bath, the mainstay of the melas. On these days, millions of ordinary pilgrims, along with sadhus and monastics, immerse themselves in the Ganga and chant invocatory mantras.

Monastic orders and akharas of sadhus usually camp at the mela grounds for the entire length of the fair. These camps are usually the site of devotional singing, rituals, and the seemingly exotic performance of austerities - such as sadhus lying on beds of nails, contorting their bodies into impossible yogic asanas, and so on. To the

uninitiated, this might appear nothing more than a freak-show. But, in reality, all these austerities and asanas have a specific purpose that is aligned with the individual's spiritual regimen.

The Kumbh and Mahakumbh Melas also underscore the time-honoured tradition of pilgrimage, which is for the common people of this land a mainstay of their the religious lives. In the centuries prior to the introduction of mechanised forms of transport pilgrims would set out on foot from their homes, usually in groups, and make for the pilgrimage spot of their choice, some simply answering to a 'calling'or to which they felt 'called' to. The Kumbh and Mahakumbh Melas, mammoth in scale and auspiciousness, were an ideal opportunity for pilgrims to plan their spiritual journey, especially the latter ones.

To this day, it is not unusual to come across peripatetic pilgrims and sadhus walking a couple of hundred kilometres to reach the site of the melas.

From left to right: The naked naga sadhus of the Juna akhara exercise after a dip during the Ardha Kumbh Mela, the halfway Kumbh in the twelve-year cycle, at Allahabad. This photograph is taken at a shahi snan, the 'royal bath', which occurs on an especially auspicious day; The faithful gather for a holy bath in the river Kshipra during the Kumbh Mela in Ujjain in 2004; A close-up of a sadhu with his face coated with ash.

Following pages: Shamanism is, in essence, 'a calling'. Individuals who are 'called' often experience illness over a prolonged time period, being prompted to seek spiritual guidance and other shamanic healers.

DIVINE SORCERERS

The Blessed Human Being

A shaman holds up an egg as part of a ritual.

Facing page: Shamans engage in rituals that facilitate a connection with realms parallel to ours, believed to be the abode of spirits. This ability to connect with supernatural realms and forces distinguishes a shaman from ordinary human beings.

In a curious etymological twist to the tale, it may be possible that the term 'shaman' came from saman, a Turkish term for an exorcist-healer, which just might have an echo of the ancient Indian word, sramana. This idea binds this latter part of the book to the first half, which outlines the history and lifestyle of the sramanas, later called sadhus, of the Indian subcontinent. Now, we turn our attention to practitioners of another kind, those who bridge the gap between the world of spirits and everyday reality.

The spirit of things – human and natural – has long intrigued human beings. Quite literally the 'breath' that animates everything, from the Latin word spiritus, the spirit has been regarded as something mysterious and intangible. The realm of the spirit, though contiguous with the worldly realm, is believed to have its own rules and language, which ordinary human beings cannot know. A shaman is therefore a special human being, either through training in a lineage of shamans, or because he or she is blessed with an innate quality, who causes a connection with other parallel realms.

Shamanism has received a New Age boost in recent times, with accounts such as those by anthropologist Carlos Castaneda, of an apprenticeship with a Mesoamerican Yaqui shaman whom he called 'Don Juan'. Though denounced as fictional by academic critics, who questioned the veracity of his claims and cited inherent discrepancies, Castaneda's books have left a lasting impact on the perception of shamanism today. For many, his writings of accessing an alternative realm of reality, which he called nagual, and living with heightened awareness, opened the door for many to an understanding of reality as a deeper whole, rather than the surface that we tend to skim in our daily lives.

For a generation disillusioned by materialism and war, which was looking for 'free love' and a psychedelic experience, Castaneda offered a knowledge of reality quite different from that of science. It was one where energies animated the universe, where the impossible became possible, if you only knew the 'way of the warrior', a metaphor for the shaman who walked the thin line between dimensions, and could alternate between them at will, if only he had subsumed his ego, which could keep him tied to the worldly self.

A photographic documentation of an annual shamanistic ritual that is conducted in the Tov province of Mongolia. The participants are nomadic people who gather together in a shaman's camp for the ritual. Ancient animist faiths use rituals set in nature to appease or invoke deities that reside there, since every bit of the landscape is considered sacred, alive, and imbued with 'spirit'.

Devils & Jinns

One of the oldest supernatural beliefs of humanity has been in the existence of malevolent forces or spirits that exist in the natural world, who if provoked, visit harm upon an individual or a community. At times, this can take the form of the spirit entering into the body of a person causing him or her to fall sick, or commit acts that they would not otherwise. Places, too, can become possessed. Houses, for instance, could be haunted by unhappy spirits of previous occupants.

Exorcism is the term for the attempt by a shaman, medicine-man, or even priests and religious clergy, to cast the offending spirit out of a victim's body, or from a place. This is usually done by invoking a 'higher power' to make the spirit uncomfortable. At times, exorcisms can take a violent turn, with the hapless victim becoming a battleground between 'good and evil'.

It is interesting to note that though its origins are shamanistic, the practice of exorcism finds a place in many major religions of the world. The better known in popular culture might be those conducted by the Roman Catholic clergy, mainly because of films like *The Exorcist* that deal with the issue and have a priest as a central character, called upon to liberate a victim from demonic possession. The fact remains that exorcism comes within the purview of the rituals of the Catholic Church, and is described, as such, in the *Rituale Romanum* an official guidebook of the Church.

In Islam there exists a belief in *jinns,* or supernatural beings, which can cause mischief like possession. They

are challenged in the name of God, and verses from the *Quran* that speak of the glory and power of God are recited during the process of exorcism.

Vajrayana Buddhism of Tibet is believed to have absorbed elements of the shamanistic, pre-Buddhist religion of the area called Bon. Exorcism in it has taken the form of subjugation of demonic spirits who were antithetical to the Buddha's dharma. In what can be seen as a narrative of the struggle between Buddhism and Bon, these spirits came to be subdued by the crusading heroes of Buddhism, usually Indian adepts. These spirits then resurfaced as protectors of the dharma, their fierceness said to have been harnessed in its cause. This could be seen as a literal parallel to the assimilation of elements of Bon into Buddhism on the Tibetan plateau.

It might be emphasised that exorcism has at times been mishandled and misused, with tragic effects. People suffering from psychiatric disorders or physical ailments like epilepsy have been thought to be possessed by evil spirits and handed over for exorcisms to priests or shamans, thereby denying them the opportunity of medical treatment. These have at times caused their condition to deteriorate, even resulting in death. Exorcism, therefore, might have been a potent tool in times when shamans also acted as healers for their communities. In present times, it is advisable to turn to more scientific methods of medical diagnoses before considering exorcisms.

Hindu dhami shamans and their apprentices known as dhangri go into a trance. They are aided and accompanied by frenzied drumming.

Facing page: The festival of Janai Purnima, held in the first week of August, is an occasion for the dhamis to exhibit their powers as healers and wise men. Here, a shaman blesses a woman seeking a boon.

TRANCE TALES

Traditionally, shamans were an integral part of the societies and tribes they lived in, and were accorded a special measure of respect because of their powers and the role they fulfilled. According to the situation, they could act as healers, diviners, soothsayers, and general solvers of problems. The basic premise on which a shaman operated, and operates, is that our everyday reality is animated by a spiritual reality, which underlies it and props it up. In this sense, what we see and cognise around us is merely the cover, the veil, and true reality is beneath its surface, available only to one who has the intuitive skills to pierce through one and reach the other.

This is a perspective that has discernible echoes of the Vedantin worldview of everyday reality as cognised by the senses and the mind being unreal, what is called 'maya' (illusion). The veil of maya, masks from us the truth that lies hidden under its veneer, which misleads us into taking it for true reality, when it is not. The shamanic belief in the energic nature of reality which can be manipulated, provided one knows how to, too, resonates with the Tantric idea of energy being the basic building block of the universe which assumes different forms according to the situations and can be moulded by the correct application of human will.

In essence, the role of the shaman is to correct imbalances in the energy, or the spirit of something which is thought to be the reason for problematic circumstances and even the cause of disease. He or she does this often by interacting with the spirit world, by entering it through a shift in consciousness which might be brought on through the use of natural and plant-based hallucinogens like cannabis, peyote, datura, and psilocybin mushrooms, among others. With the ingestion of such a substance, the shaman enters an alternative state of consciousness, a shamanic trance and is thought to have travelled to another dimension of reality.

Once the trance has been induced, the shaman is supposed to assume another body, a sort of subtle body, or an animal or bird form and embark on his travels. In this subtle body, he can travel the spirit world, often under the supervision of a 'spirit guide'. It can be contended that shamans' trance flights are 'out of body experiences', brought on by the effects of psychotropic substances. In fact, there exist in South America lines marked into the landscape, either remarkably straight or in recognisable shapes, that are associated with the shamanic flight into the spirit world.

Most notable amongst these are the Nazca Lines in Peru, built between the fifth and seventh centuries AD. Discovered from airplanes flying above the region in the 1930s, the figures and shapes are spread over an area of eighty kilometres, with the largest drawing measuring 200 meters across. These were created by clearing the top soil in these shapes, and have been preserved due to the arid climate of the plateau on which they are located.

Though they have been studied extensively since their discovery, no suitable explanation has been given for their existence, that of use by shamans during their flights being the more plausible one. This could be true given the fact that they are really meant to be seen from above the ground, and could have been created as a guide map for shamans on their purported flights to the netherworld.

Above and facing page: Shamans connect with the realm of the spirit, which, though contiguous with the worldly realm, is believed to have its own rules and language that ordinary human beings cannot know. The shaman can enter this realm using specific rituals.

HEALER OF SOULS

What used to at one time be referred to as 'medicine men' are also shamans, in their role as healers of the sick, and not just physically, but mentally, emotionally

A form that resembles a candelabra in the desert in Paracas, Peru, related to the Nazca Lines. Though they have been studied extensively since their discovery, no suitable explanation has been given for their existence.

An elder at a temple in Manali greets two shamans from Goshal village during the Dussehra festivities. Flowers are offered, smoke from a sacred fire purifies the area, the temple bell is sounded and prayers are said. Puja rituals, prayer and dancing are part of the festival.

Facing page: A Nepalese shaman, known as a Jhankari, wears traditional clothes and offers a boiled egg to a patient in order to drive off evil spirits.

Following pages: Shamans are believed to be messengers between the human and spirit worlds.

and spiritually as well. Because sickness is believed to be caused due to an imbalance in the energy or soul quality of a human being, the shaman undertakes a journey into the spirit world to retrieve elements that will make the soul of the sick whole and balanced again. In some cases, the shaman must go through the experience of a grievous illness himself so as to become able to heal another.

In many shamanic cultures, one of the reasons for illness is believed to be the possession of an individual by demonic or evil spirits. In such cases, the shaman acts as an exorcist who casts the offending spirit out of the individual. Exorcism is also practised by members of the Catholic Church and is seen as a battle for the victim's soul – with the priest supposedly acting on behalf of God to claim the soul on the side of 'good', and the possessing spirit is considered almost always to be a demon and evil.

In shamanic cultures, a variety of psychological and physical diseases might be attributed to malevolent spirits having entered the victim and stolen his or her true self. The shaman must then enact rites and rituals to cast the demon out, which may require burning purifying substances, using empowered talismans, and generally making the demonic spirit uncomfortable in its habitation of the victim. The shaman must also make the demon yield up the victim's soul and have it in place so he or she can return to normal life.

The shaman's role as healer encompasses aspects other than exorcism, and can mean providing healing through energy, plant and herbs. It must be said here

Dhami shamans gather in a shrine in the forest to make offerings to protector deities. Instead of live sheep, its wool is being offered in a symbolic sacrifice.

Facing page: A dhami shaman in a trance at Naumuli, 'source of nine springs', in Nepal – a popular spot to summon spirits and make predictions. The place is considered to be sacred. According to folklore, a powerful deity travels through the springs from Lake Manasarovar to Mount Kailash.

that in each society, different shamans might specialize in different branches of healing – those that are exorcists might not be energy healers, and so on. Once the problem has been identified, the victim can approach the shaman who would be most appropriate for his or her healing.

Healing by transforming energy is a fundamental belief in most shamanistic cultures. Because energy is believed to be present everywhere, and the individual spirit is also seen as being made of this universal energy, anything that causes a blockage or distortion in the natural flow of energy will lead to the manifestation of disease. During an energy healing, a shaman will attempt to, in simple terms, rid the individual of 'bad energy', or a blockage that impedes the flow of energy, and replace it with good or wholesome energy. If it is a blockage, the shaman will work towards restoring a vital, healthy flow.

Another method of healing practised in shamanic cultures is what has been termed as 'soul retrieval'. Shamanic teacher Sandra Ingerman explains in her book, Soul Retrieval: Mending the Fragmented Self (Harper, San Francisco, 1991), 'Whenever we experience trauma, a part of our vital essence separates from us in order to survive the experience by escaping the full impact of the pain.' This is conceptually a loss of a part of one's soul, which lessens one's vital energy and also can lead to disease.

How can one understand the concept of loss of pieces of one's soul?

A shamanistic rite in progress on the banks of the startlingly blue Lake of Manasarovar. The shaman has entered a trance, and his assistant is translating his pronouncements for the benefit of their companions.

Psychologically, we could perhaps think of it as a human survival strategy – we attempt to withdraw from what is unpleasant or painful. In doing so, we might 'leave' a part of us behind in the sense of disassociating from an experience that is part of our self and our life's journey. This fragments our psyche and we are not as whole or centred anymore as we might have been had we been able to integrate that experience in our lives.

In shamanic terms, we have lost some of our vital energy in allowing our psyche to become fragmented. This is talked about in the sense of losing a part of our spirit, and the shaman's endeavour must be to help us heal that loss and become whole again. In order to do this, we must learn to accept the reality of what happened, and then perhaps consciously let go of that pain. So that we have that part of our spirit back, but with a sense of wholeness, and wellness.

Much like the phenomenon of wind from high pressure areas rushing in to low pressure areas causing storms in its wake, it is believed that when part of the spirit is lost, the space it leaves empty can become filled with any kind of energy, which might also be negative. It can be felt in the common experience during periods of sadness of not feeling like oneself.

One of the ways in which some cultures where shamanism is practised identified a loss of soul, was when somebody stopped singing. It was so much a part of their daily lives that when a person would not sing, it immediately was taken as a sign of something not being right. And conversely, when they began singing again, it meant they were healed and whole again.

POWERS OF DIVINATION

In his book, Shamanism, Archaic Techniques of Ecstasy (Bollingen Series LXXVI, Pantheon Books, New York, 1964), scholar Mircea Eliade enumerates certain factors that are common to shamans all over the world. Along with the ability to heal, entered altered states of consciousness, go on spirit journeys, and invoke spirit guides, Eliade includes the powers of divination. Whatever their method of choice might be – reading runes, throwing bones, tarot cards, or anything else – shamans can, or certainly claim to, foretell the future.

From helping recover lost cattle or children to predicting the outcome of crops or hunts, shamans are called upon to help the community navigate their lives. Shamanic divination is based on the concept of a non-linear concept of time

Following pages: Acting as mediators in their culture, shamans communicate with the spirits on behalf of their community, including the spirits of the deceased.

A Buddhist lama along with local shamans at a burial ground near Mount Kailash. Due to the deep belief in the sacredness of Mount Kailash and its surroundings, this is considered to be an especially auspicious spot to die, as well as to renounce worldly life.

A nun rests for a while during her prostrations around Mount Kailash. She is suffering from sunburn on her face. Her hands and body are covered with a coarse canvas cloth for protection.

Facing page: A shaman stands by to make way for Tibetan pilgrims who are prostrating their way to the base of Mount Kailash – considered to be an exceedingly meritorious and pious activity.

where past, present and future co-exist in the same continuum, but separated by divisions. The shaman is able to penetrate the boundaries between the contiguous planes of time to gather the knowledge that is required to make the divination.

The actual process of divination is shrouded in mystery, decipherable only to the initiates. However there is enough known about the different methods and tools that are used by shamans to give us an idea of how they go about predicting, or rather knowing, the future. One such method uses a rock to answer questions, and is a fascinating blend of imagination, awareness and intuitive knowing. In this, the individual is asked by the shaman to not tell him or her about the problem, but focus on it intently and go out in search of a rock. He or she must, while looking for the rock, keep the question steadily in their minds, and must pick up the rock that somehow conveys to them its suitability for divination.

A shaman, with a shaved forehead, wearing several strings of rudraksha beads, conducts a ritual.

Facing page: A shaman in a trance licks a hot poker and drinks steaming oil to demonstrate the strength of his spirit possession during a pilgrimage to Kailash-Manasarovar.

This rock is then brought to the shaman who quite literally communes with it. The questioner is asked to repeat his or her question several times while the shaman sits with the rock and enters a kind of meditative absorption. It is said that each facet of the rock opens up a point of entry into another zone of reality for the shaman. As the shaman progresses into it, details related to the problem emerge.

Another interesting divination practice is that where the shaman assumes specific postures and meditates on the question at hand. The shaman will sit in these postures accompanied by a rhythmic sound, that of a drum or a rattle or any other instrument. When an answer emerges in his or her mind, he releases his body from the posture and 'comes back'. Sometimes, an answer might not appear as an answer but a vision might emerge in the mind which the shaman will then decipher all possible meanings for before sharing with the questioner.

An even more seemingly esoteric method is that of divining with sunbeams. It

is essentially a visualisation exercise that has as its purpose finding out the location of something that has been misplaced or lost, including people, and also to locate game for hunters. In this, the shaman lay down in seclusion, with drumming in the background to help him or her achieve a heightened state of awareness.

He or she visualised that they were in the open, complete with feeling the wind, and the sensation of walking. They then looked up into the sky, into the sun, while focusing on the question they sought the location for, even supplicating the sun for help. A sunbeam would become brighter and the shaman's task was to follow this beam, even flying across the terrain if need be. Where the beam touched the earth was the location that was being searched for. Upon emerging from the trance, the shaman would describe the exact place and it would be found.

Divination can be thought of as a method of diagnosis, as well as an art of deciphering signs for hidden meaning. It makes use of the human faculty of imagination, which according to the scientific rational worldview, is not a reliable source of information. For the shaman, it is the prime source of information, and is the gateway into altered states of consciousness that lead him or her to what to them is the most authentic information possible.

Interpreting natural occurrences is an important part of shamanic divination. In indigenous shamanic cultures, all natural phenomena and beings familiar to them are accorded pre-decided meanings. In this way, they have already been designated as portents, and the way they behave on a particular occasion is interpreted by the shaman according to that particular context. For instance, if an eagle is a symbol of positive power, and if it appears in the sky circling, or swooping, it could be interpreted as a specific message to the tribe – perhaps their spiritual energy is waning, perhaps they need to undertake a collective rite, and so on. Deciphering portents requires of the shaman careful observation of the phenomenon in question and application of his or her own wisdom to it.

To do this, the shaman must be sharply attuned to the natural environment, as well as the energic reality that powers everything around. Their skills must combine acute perception of the seen as well as the unseen, that which is apparent and that which is hidden.

NEW AGE SHAMANISM

With the disappearance of their habitats and livelihoods, and the replacement of the old worldview that found mystery and sacredness in everything around with the modern, scientific, rational worldview, the practice of traditional shamanism has become increasingly rare. Because it was so deeply rooted in the area the community lived in, the loss of place, and the shrinking of natural spaces, took away the shaman's ability to connect with nature on a one-on-one basis.

Dislocation of communities also led to their fragmentation and dispersal, which took away from the shaman the very ground on which he or she practised their craft. Without nature, and without the tribe who banded around the shaman and aided the soul journeys and the rituals, there seemed to be no point for the shaman to exist any longer. Also, as newer generations received a modern education, they had no time or interest in spending years apprenticing in traditional knowledge systems, including that of the shaman.

Facing page: In Sikkim, a Lepcha along with shaman uses beer made from millet and other enticing offerings to capture spirits.

Traditional shamanism does continue in those areas of the world that are still remote and relatively inaccessible, and are yet not completely assimilated into

the 'modern world'. Mainstream society in most places might have little use for shamanistic knowledge, seeing it as superstition, or just being unable to connect with a worldview that is so removed from the scientific and materialistic view of reality that we are conditioned into believing completely.

However, there has been a revival of shamanism in New Age circles, and though it may not always be the 'real deal' based on an ancient cultural practice, the endeavour is to at least adopt the worldview and some practices of cultural shamans, and use them as tools to enhance the quality of one's life. This could potentially be criticised for taking practices and beliefs out of their cultural contexts, as well as for changing the intention with which they were undertaken, which in turn had an impact on its meaning – for instance, instead of using a spirit journey for healing or entering a heightened state of awareness, it is used for de-stressing. Or, the use of ritual psychotropic substances, for just getting high, which reduces it to a drug, as habit-forming and harmful as any other recreational drug.

These arguments against the new wave of shamanism can also be employed against the use of other ancient forms of knowledge and wisdom in modern contexts as well, with yoga being a prime example. Can the intention with which Patanjali, who wrote the definitive treatise on yoga in the second century BCE, the Yogasutra, practised yoga be compared with that of a young person who goes to yoga class in New York or even in New Delhi in the twenty-first century? The truth is that times have changed, as have contexts and realities, and if we are to make any use of traditional and ancient wisdom, it will have to be done in the light of today.

There has been a burgeoning interest in the last few years in wicca, neo-shamanism, paganism and magick around the world, and what these have in common is a sensibility that can be traced to shamanistic cultures. Wicca, for instance, takes its inspiration from pre-Christian religions of Europe that had powerful women practitioners, or witches, who were later denounced and hounded out of society with the ascendancy of the Catholic Church.

Wicca has been used in recent decades to create a community, a 'sisterhood', where women can explore a spirituality that honours their femininity, helps them connect more deeply with themselves and others, and brings them in touch with the sacred dimension of life and nature. A lot of women who sign up to be 'witches' find it a liberating and empowering experience.

Neo-shamanism is often a collection of beliefs and practices from different shamanistic traditions that have been brought together by a practitioner or teacher with the aim of helping his or her students through their spiritual growth processes. An interesting way of looking at how neo-shamanism differs from traditional shamanism is to see the latter as a way of gathering knowledge, while the former is more about the experience itself and not so much about the need for getting something out of it. So, for instance, if a traditional shaman is on a spirit journey, it is with some express motivation – to bring back lost parts of the soul, or to heal, and so on. While in neo-shamanism, just the act of going on a spirit journey would be the goal.

While the authentic shaman might be endangered, much like the environment he inhabited and the lifestyle that gave rise to him, shamanism as a way of knowing and experiencing the world has received a second life. If not so much in form, it definitely survives in spirit.

Facing page: A group of wiccans dance in the nave of an old church during a ceremony near Amsterdam in the Netherlands. Rooted in pre-Christian paganism, wicca has been used in recent decades to create a 'sisterhood' where women can explore a spirituality that honours their femininity, helps them connect more deeply with themselves and others, and brings them in touch with the sacred dimension of life and nature.

SHAMANS OF THE SUBCONTINENT

Diversity Redefined

A monolithic stone shrine in Mao district of Manipur.

Facing page: A group of shamans washes in a mountain stream. Animism is an essential part of shamanism. It deems all life and nature as sacred, and sees them permeated with a divine life-force. It is thought to be the earliest religion that human beings developed on the basis of their observation of their surroundings.

The Indian subcontinent has provided fertile ground and inspiration for not just spiritual sadhana, but for the growth and development of diverse philosophies, sciences, cultures, music, dance, foods, fabrics, and so on. The sheer multiplicity in evidence in the subcontinent is mindboggling, and not just in terms of range but depth too. If we study any of these, the centuries of deep thought, contributed by successive generations that have watered and nurtured that particular aspect of culture or philosophy, will become evident.

Shamanism, as practiced in the Indian subcontinent, has primitive roots that lead back into time, perhaps to the point when human beings first began to live in communities. Or at least to the time its oldest civilization came into being – the Indus Valley Civilization – that flourished across large swathes of the northern and western parts of the subcontinent from approximately 3300 BCE to 1900 BCE. Though not much is known about the civilization, it has been conjectured that it had a cult of the worship of the mother goddess because of the recovery of a large number of images depicting her.

Along with propitiating the mother goddess, which has been identified with the earth mother because of the fact that the inhabitants were primarily farmers, the recovery of a large number of animal figures points to the possibility of some kind of animistic worship too.

ORIGINAL ANIMISM

Animism is an essential part of shamanism, though it might not be its only constituent. In simple terms, animism deems all life and nature as sacred, and sees them permeated with a divine life-force, and is thought of as being the earliest religion that human beings developed on the basis of their observation of their surroundings. The earliest human beings lived in nature and so experienced it keenly.

Phenomena like rain, thunder, volcanoes, fires, earthquakes, the cycle of seasons, even the periodicity of sunrise and sunset, must have invoked a certain

A seal excavated from the ruins of the Indus Valley Civilization. The recovery of a large number of animal figures from its ruins points to the possibility of some kind of animistic worship as having been practised therein.

Facing pages: A group of Nyishi women in Arunachal Pradesh participate in a group dance to propitiate deities for a good harvest. They carry their woven cane baskets in the ritual dance, as symbols of the work done at the time of harvest.

degree of awe, as would have the animals, big and small, that shared their habitat and were either to be feared or hunted for food. As they began to discover the possibilities of planting things instead of merely plucking and gathering them from the forests, they must have experienced the miracle of birth, of life emerging, reminiscent of the emergence of their own young into the world.

This feeling of awe and wonder came twinned with fear, and the very real possibility of danger, injury and death. As hunter-gatherer, the early human had little means of safeguarding himself against animal attacks and natural calamities, and sometimes no guarantee of finding the right kind of animals he was equipped to hunt. Later, as he began to farm, and grew dependant for sustenance on the yield of the earth, he found he would not survive if his crops did not, which could happen for any number of reasons – lack of rain or an over-abundance of it, unseasonal hailstorms, pestilence and crop diseases.

If his feelings of awe did not convince him of 'higher' forces, his fear certainly did. And these forces were unpredictable. They could strike at will, at any time, without warning, and everything could change, life could end. Born of this fragility and helplessness was a need to have at least some say in his destiny, even if he did so as a supplicant to the higher powers. At least he could invoke benevolence, put the powers in a good mood with gifts, like animal sacrifices and offerings of his precious grain and fruit, and hope their malevolence would be quietened and instead, they would grant him his survival as a boon.

In fact, because of the lifestyles of their tribes and communities which remained close to that of the early hunter-gatherers and farmers, one of the tasks of the shaman was to divine the presence and location of appropriate prey, invoke rain for crops, predict drought and other unfavourable circumstances and prescribe remedies for them.

Animism is essentially non-anthropomorphic. The human being is not at the centre of the animistic universe, and he is certainly not greater or more important than all other constituents of nature. Animism sees the created universe as a network of inter-relationships, where everything is in essence spirit and interconnected with one another. Hence, everything must be accorded equal respect, whether animate or inanimate.

Many of the beliefs central to later shamanistic cultures owe their origin to animism. This includes propitiatory rituals, designed to invoke the goodwill of the spirits, thought to govern that which was essential to life. This also led to something we can refer to as 'sacred landscaping', which meant that the features of the landscape of the tribe's habitat were accorded their individual myths that made them relevant to the larger story of the sacred universe of the tribe.

So, for instance, the big waterfall close by could have been the site of a creation myth, or made as a result of the happenings in it. And the rocks were the bones of ancient creatures that were sleeping and were not to be disturbed or awakened, for who knows what havoc they might wreak then. The trees could have spirits that lived in them and who could, when hungry, devour the soul of a weary traveller who stopped to lie under it. And the rains came astride the bow of a god, who needed to shoot them to the earth as arrows, the bow becoming visible at the end of the shower as a rainbow. And so on.

This process of sacralisation through myths was accompanied usually by the necessity to propitiate the spirit aspects thus created. The rain god had to be

A nyubu, an Apatani shaman, prays at a shrine erected for the dead in an attempt to drive away evil spirits. A sacrificed chicken hangs next to him. The Apatani bury their dead, sometimes in a fenced garden on family land. A bamboo shrine is erected therein, and animals are sacrificed as offerings to the deceased.

Chotrol Tenzin Wangdrak Karsang Rinpoche, a native of Kham in Tibet, is the foremost luminary of Bon in western Tibet.

supplicated to pick up his bow and shoot forth the rains, for instance. And some phenomena needed to be pacified, like giants that rumbled in the belly of the earth and caused earthquakes, or the ancient creatures that slept in the bony rocks of the landscape. This need for supplication was met by the resident shaman of the tribe.

The earliest Vedic civilization is thought to be animistic in part due to its emphasis on the propitiation of gods related to natural phenomena, though the culture that started off practising it veered towards other philosophies in time. The Rig Vedic compendium of hymns for ritual propitiations is proof of the animistic nature of the early Vedic people.

BONS OF TIBET

Bon is the faith that was prevalent in Tibet in the pre-Buddhist era, and is predominantly shamanistic and animist in nature. After the introduction of Buddhism in the seventh century AD in the Tibetan plateau, Bon lost its position as primary religion, though it has been suggested that it seeped into the practice

Yongdzin Lopon Tenzin Namdak Rimpoche, one of the senior most teachers of Tibet's Bon tradition today, is seen here wearing his ceremonial hat. He founded the Triten Norbutse monastery in Kathmandu, Nepal, in 1987 to preserve Bon teachings.

Facing page: Geshe Gelek Jinpa, a doctor of Bon theology, performs a ritual. Bon is the pre-Buddhist faith of Tibet, and is predominantly shamanistic and animist in nature. It is thought that several Bon practices steeped into Tibetan Buddhism over the centuries, giving it a unique cultural flavour.

of Vajrayana Buddhism over the centuries. This added a unique flavour to the Buddhism of Tibet, and made it distinct from its Indian parent, as well as cultural siblings elsewhere in the world.

It is interesting to note that most of what exists as Bon today, is an evolutionary branch known as Yungdrung Bon, which unlike shamanistic cultures, traces its origin to a single person – Tonpa Shenrab Miwache. This is quite like Buddhism, which also owes its beginning to one individual, Gautama the Buddha. And like the Buddha, Tonpa Shenrab's words were also not recorded by him but were only put down as scripture after his death. It is believed that he did the sadhana requisite for enlightenment in a spiritual realm called Tagzig Olmo Lung Ring, a Shambhala-esque land that has been physically located in the vicinity of Mount Kailash in Tibet.

Upon the successful completion of his sadhana, Tonpa Shenrab is said to have promised the god of compassion, Shenlha Okar, that he would return to the earthly realm and help people in their spiritual journeys. This does sound very close to the bodhisattva ideal of Tibetan Buddhism, where the Buddha-to-be defers personal enlightenment for the sake of all other beings. Since most of the history of Bon was formally recorded only in the tenth century AD, after the ascendancy of Buddhism, a certain contamination of the former with the latter is assumed.

The Bon scriptures, as they exist today, include the Sutras and Tantras like all schools of Tibetan Buddhism, and in addition have the 'Perfection of Wisdom' teachings, and 'Knowledge' teachings, the last of which are seen to have some similarity in teachings in the Nyingma school of Tibetan Buddhism. These form the core philosophy of the religion, which is then embellished with a lot of practical know-how, which includes knowledge of magical rituals, divination, craft, medicine, poetry and art, among other things, which might belong to the tool-box of the indigenous shaman.

The teachings attributed to Tonpa Shenrab, too, are a mix of shamanistic practices and aspects that have either gone from Bon to Tibetan Buddhism, or equally possibly the other way round. Among the four principal streams of knowledge, 'White Water' has directions of dealing with esoteric aspects of reality, 'Black Water' is related to magic, funerals and ransom rituals, 'Land of Phan' details philosophy, and 'Divine Guide' comprises the teachings known as Dzogchen, the path to returning to the primordial, original state of mind. Dzogchen is a body of teachings that are held in high esteem in the Tibetan Buddhist worldview as well, which in turn shows the extent of commingling that resulted in the appearance of Yungdrung Bon.

Yungdrung Bon has as its primary sacred symbol a left-facing swastika, called yungdrung and from which the tradition probably received its name, as opposed to a right-facing one which is common to both Hinduism and Theravada Buddhism. While the primary symbol of Tibetan Buddhism is the dorje, Sanskrit 'vajra', which stands for the 'thunderbolt vehicle' to enlightenment – Vajrayana.

The fact that the shamanistic practices of older Bon continued in Yungdrung Bon as part of the main religion, as opposed to being relegated to the peripheries of Tibetan Buddhism, distinguishes the two wisdom traditions of Tibet. These practices include divination, ways of controlling the weather, dealing with spirits to effect healing, and so on.

Facing page: Abbot of the Triten Norbutse monastery, Khenpo Tenpa Yungdrung Rinpoche, poses with student-monks. The monastery in Kathmandu is one of the two main Bon monasteries outside of Tibet.

The cult of blood sacrifices that existed in the old Bon religion came to be frowned upon by Buddhism, and was abandoned by a section of Bon priests. These came to be known as followers of 'White Bon'. Those who continued to make animal sacrifices were rather ominously classified as 'Black Bon'.

One of the most prominent and visible symbols of assimilation of the old Bon practices into Tibetan Buddhism is the institution of the Nechung Oracle, which is the official oracle of the Dalai Lamas and is consulted on all important matters, personal and political, by them. The fourteenth Dalai Lama, Tenzin Gyatso, famously asked the Nechung Oracle about the feasibility of getting out of Lhasa in 1959 and going to India, and decided upon that course of action once he had received the Oracle's assent.

The story of the origin of the Nechung Oracle could be seen as a metaphor for Buddhism's endeavour towards assimilating the pre-existing religion of the plateau, rather than replacing or destroying it, and using it in an assisting role to consolidate its own position. According to the mythology of Tibetan Buddhism, the great guru from India, Padmasambhava, who consolidated Buddhism in Tibet, performed a ritual dance at the site of the Samye monastery to rid the location of disturbing spirits. During the dance, he is said to have gained control of the spirit, Pehar, who agreed to become a protector of the dharma from then on. Pehar is said to have manifested as the deity, Dorje Drakden, who as the Nechung Oracle became a protector and oracular advisor of the Dalai Lamas.

The actual prediction ceremony of the Nechung Oracle has been witnessed and described in recent times in detail by the Dalai Lama himself in his book, Freedom In Exile. The kuten (the physical medium of the oracle) is dressed in an elaborate costume for the ceremony, and wears a mirror on his chest, thought to symbolise the quality of the original mind, or dzogchen. His attire includes a huge headdress that is put on when he enters a trance. The trance is induced through drumming and chanting, and once the spirit possession occurs, the Oracle goes into a trance, during which he or the spirit in residence, answers the questions that are put to him.

Nechung is among the many oracles that are used by Tibetans to not just divine the future, but also to heal afflictions of body and mind.

TRANS-HIMALAYAN SHAMANS

The Gurung people, who live in the Nepal Himalayas, have a shamanistic tradition that is very similar to the old Bon shamanism of Tibet. It is believed that what they practise has much more in common with the pre-Buddhist Bon than the later version of Bon that developed in Tibet after the advent of Buddhism. This could be possible since the Gurungs migrated from Tibet to Nepal in the sixth century, just before Buddhism changed the Bon cosmos forever.

In a sense, one could say that the original Bon has been preserved by the Gurung shamans. For instance, the practices of ancestor worship, and the performance of sacrificial blood rituals that were banned by the 'White Bon', continued among the Gurungs. The Paju shamans of the Gurungs are concerned with matters of life including divination, spirit possession, exorcism, and so on, while the Ghyabre shamans are responsible for rituals associated with death and shepherding the souls of the dead.

The Gurung shamans maintain that they continue to possess extraordinary powers such as influencing the weather, causing landslides, and so on, which the Tibetan Buddhist priests have lost. Many such powers or 'siddhis' are outlined in the literature of both Tibetan Buddhism, and Indian Tantric lore as well. The landscape of the Gurung shamans is populated with spirits of trees, lakes, forests, mountains, and they attempt to keep them appeased and well-disposed to them and the community. Blood sacrifices are part of this attempt. Gurung shamans also act as mediums between this world and the spirits, and like the Nechung Oracle, can go into trance to find answers to specific questions put to them by the community.

A Bon teacher, Khenpo Lungtok Tenpai Nyima Rinpoche, blessing two women at the Tashi Menriling Monastery in Dolanji, India. Like the dominant tradition of Tibet – Vajrayana Buddhism – Bon teachers and adherents too, left Tibet in large numbers after the Chinese invasion and the Dalai Lama's escape in 1959.

There are other minor tribes of similar extraction as the Gurungs, who live in

Tamang shamans from Nepal dance to the beat of their handheld drums. The Tamangs have a dual clergy – Buddhist priests for rites of passage, and shamans for healing and anything else related with the spirit world.

the high reaches of the Himalayas and practise a version of the old Bon religion. These include the Thakali, the Magars, and the Tamangs in Nepal. The latter have a two-fold clergy system – Buddhist priests for rites of passage, and shamans for healing and other matters thought to be related to the spirit world.

Among Tamang shamans, initiation is a long and arduous process. The individual might become possessed at first, and is then driven to a kind of madness where he runs away into the wilderness and lives in nature. This phase lasts until he can understand his calling and begin to try and gain control over the powers that supposedly well up within him. At this point, a guru or teacher is necessary to guide the initiate through the process of making sense of the spirit world, which now calls out to him. He must also become adept at entering the trance state at will, and of summoning his spirit guide, who is necessary for him to make the journey into the dimension of the spirit.

It has been recorded that there used to exist a shamanistic religion in the areas

of Gilgit-Baltistan, currently in Pakistan, which was rooted out after the advent of Islam in the fourteenth century AD. The shamans of this area were known as bitan, and there has been discerned a similarity between their practices and those of the old Bon shamanism. The bitan performed rituals to spirits of the mountain whom they referred to as pari, which they believed inhabited the entire region, and offered them sacrifices of goat's blood, which the bitan too imbibed. They also entered trances, brought on by the inhalation of smoke from burning juniper wood, in order to communicate with the pari.

The pari were believed to inhabit high altitude areas, like mountain peaks and the valleys and meadows around them. They could be aggressive and malevolent, and were often blamed for altitude sickness, snowstorms, and avalanches. The bitan were supposed to be able to propitiate the pari through specific rituals, and when in a good mood, the pari could enable the community or the individual to good fortune.

Apparently, anybody could not just choose to become a bitan, like one can a doctor or a teacher. It was not a vocation, but a calling, something that seems to be common to all shamanistic cultures. Perhaps since it is a demanding, time-consuming vocation, in fact you can never stop being a shaman, it cannot be done by anybody who has not felt 'the call'.

The called bitan would first receive some hints of his or her (they used to be from both genders) specialness as a child, usually from the way animals behaved around them, or from other strange natural occurrences. Then, at some point in adolescence, a pari would appear to them and they would realize their calling. They would then suffer from an illness, which could become worse if they refused to respond to the call of the pari. If they did, the pari would again appear to them and begin their process of learning.

The bitan were the community's spokespersons with the pari, the via media who both interceded on behalf of his fellow community members and conveyed back to them the will of the pari. They were therefore summoned in case of any calamity or misfortune that was thought to have been caused by supernatural agencies, as well as asked to invoke good luck before beginning a new venture or during a rite of passage. The pari were not the only spirits the bitan had to be careful about. There were demonic spirits on the prowl, called shiatus, who would haunt specific areas like graveyards, and who could attack the bitan.

It has been recorded that the bitan would sometimes act as political

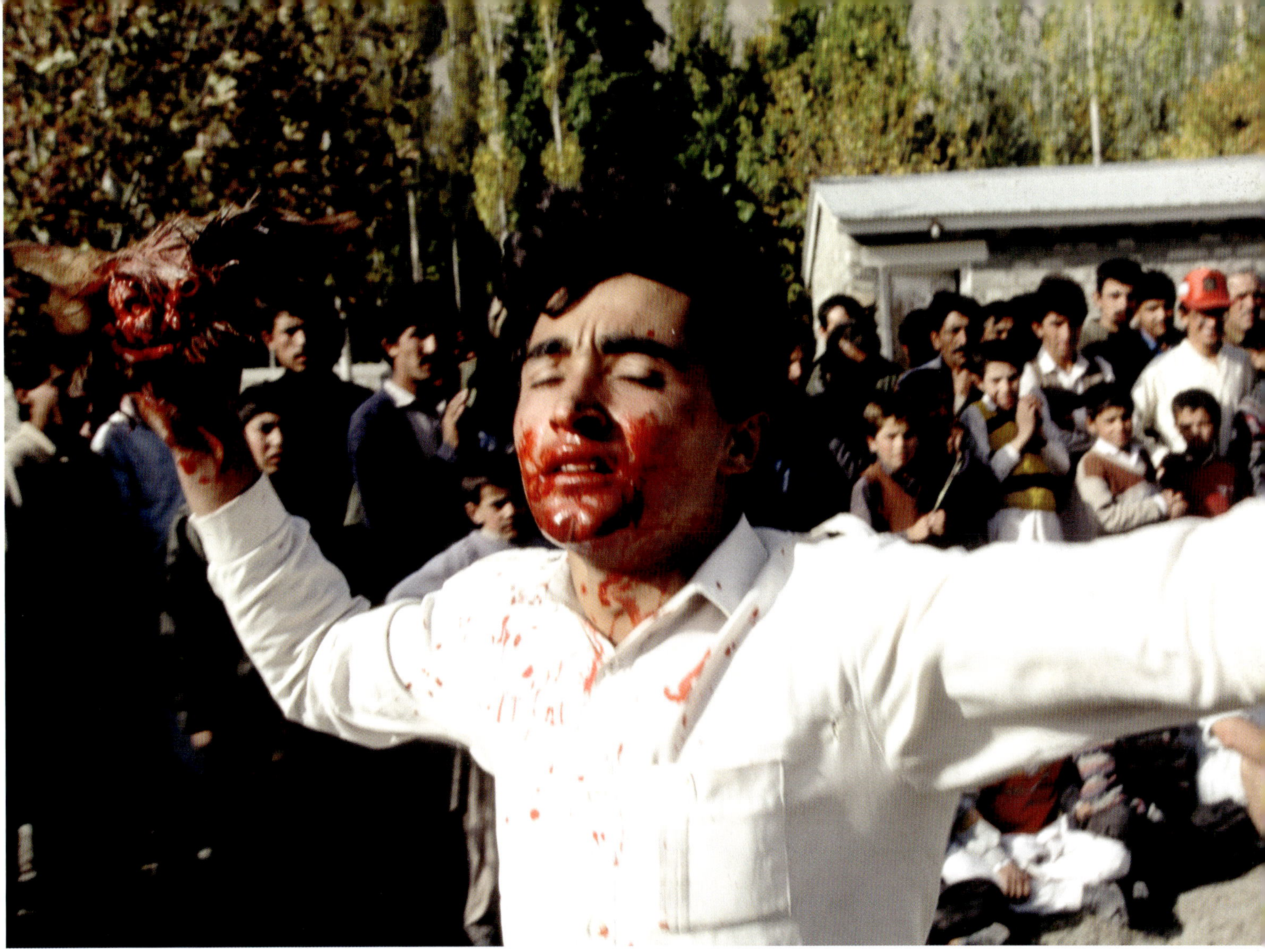

soothsayers, protesting unjust laws or taxes on behalf of the people to the rulers. Because they did this in the name of the pari, they were not penalised, and it was a way of raising contentious issues. Now, this 'paranormal' form of protest, along with the institution of the bitan, is a thing of the past.

Above and facing page: A bitan enters a trance with the aid of juniper smoke, dance, and a blood sacrifice, in Aliabad in the Hunza Valley in Pakistan. Bitans are local shamans, who go into trance to convey the will of paris, or 'mountain fairies', who speak through them.

MEITEI OF MANIPUR

The Meitei are the dominant community in the north-eastern state of Manipur in India. Though they are predominantly Hindu in the Vaishnava tradition that is the cult of the adoration of Vishnu, a robust practice of shamanism exists alongside and informs their lives. Meitei shamans are both male and female, referred to as maiba and maibi respectively. Both have their roles predetermined, and stick to their areas of influence and work.

Like the Tamang shamans and the bitan, the maibi are called to their vocation, but interestingly, it is not so for the maiba. Any man can choose to be a maiba and study with a teacher. Maibas are mostly entrusted with the task of healing and administering medicine, and because the local medical system has been recorded in a text, the Maibarol, it is available for reference, should the practitioner require it.

It is the women shamans in Manipur who perform the heroic shamanic tasks – going into trance, making divinations, communing with the spirits. Perhaps in this sense, one could conjecture that theirs is the more important role from a shamanic perspective. They are the authentic shamans, who must follow the call

A Meitei maibi of Manipur: Maibis, women shamans, are 'called' to their vocation through an illness, and must then apprentice with a senior maibi who will over time teach her to enter trance states, connect with spirits, and learn to translate knowledge gained in the spirit world for healing and divination.

they receive – whether it is from the spirits, a divine being, or their own selves.

The way the call to become a maibi manifests is through an illness, that refuses to be healed. Typically,all systems of medicine are tried without success. As the woman wastes away, she realizes what the reason is, and calls in a maiba who will treat her. She must then leave off her ordinary life and go to apprentice with a senior maibi, who will over time teach her to enter and hold trance states, connect with spirits, and learn to translate knowledge gained in the spirit world into that which is meaningful and useful in ordinary reality.

Many maibis continue to live regular, married lives, though they have been known to give up that option as well. For, it seems, despite the respect that they obviously command in Manipuri society, there are many families who will not want a maibi as part of their ranks. The reason is perhaps the same that has kept women out of the whole adventure of spiritual seeking for all these centuries, even as men have had the license to get up and leave their lives and their relationships behind.

The very idea of a woman taking off independently on a spiritual quest poses a threat to the status quo in a patriarchal society, as does a woman who is empowered, who will not accept the status quo just because she should, or is required to do so by convention. The moment a maibi is 'chosen' or 'called', her spiritual quest has begun. She must honour the call of the spirit over and above the diktats of society. She is, in that sense, a woman unshackled from gender roles and expectations, and is free to travel and work, as she chooses, or as the need arises. And so, she becomes a square peg in a round hole, difficult to fit into conventions, and yet bound to society because her work is amidst its babble and concerns.

On the whole, Meitei shamanism is unique because it has a written scriptural basis. This is actually not just true about their shamanism but also about every other aspect of life, which was recorded in written documents called puya, which were meticulously written and updated from the fifteenth century onwards. The subjects include medicine, art, science, astrology, and so on.

Maibas and maibis continue to practise their craft in present times despite a dwindling clientele and the inroads made by modernity. It is still customary in Manipur to invite a maibi to cut a new-born baby's umbilical cord and invite its 'shadow soul' to enter. And maibas are called in to confirm and announce a death.

APATANI OF ARUNACHAL

The Apatani people of Arunachal Pradesh follow a distinct shamanistic culture with animist overtones, which is known as the 'Donyi Polo' religion. Donyi Polo refers to the sun and moon, with the former associated with feminine energy, and the latter with masculine. They are worshipped as the guardian deities deputed by Bo and Bomong, the supreme beings. Donyi Polo are manifest and visible, whereas the supreme beings are not.

The Donyi Polo religion is animistic to the extent that it advocates an equality of all beings, where none are superior to the other and all have their own place in the order of life. There is a host of accompanying protector deities as well, who are supposed to keep the adherents on the correct, virtuous path, and keep them from going astray.

The Apatani also trace their ancestry to Abotani, a kind of primordial man, who is actually a shared ancestor with all the Tani people – the Nishi, Tagin, Hill Miri and the Adi. The term 'Abotani' literally means 'human father', and he is supposed to have brought the technique of rice farming to the Tani people. The story of how he did that is replete with references to Abotani's quick-wittedness, which ultimately saves the day and helps him attain new staple crops – rice, maize and millet.

The story goes something like this: Abotani went to Takar-Taji's place where a wedding feast was in progress. Abotani tricked the latter into sacrificing only one 'mithun' (Indian bison), which proved inadequate for the guests. As a result, Abotani's dog and a deer found only a packet of soya seeds to eat. Unhappy about it, they fought with each other and ran away, with Abotani following them.

After many days of chasing one another, the three landed in the realm of the Digo Ane, 'keepers of the land', where they were promptly arrested. After some time, when no hope was in sight, Abotani again played a trick. He placed a dead rat in his armpit and pretended to be on the verge of death. Scared lest his tribe would come and harass them if he died, the Digo Ane set him free and gifted him with seeds of rice, millet and maize. This is how the Apatani believe these crops came to them.

The Donyi Polo religion has a shamanistic aspect in the sense that there is a prevalent belief in the spirits that inhabit all aspects of the landscape, and who must be appeased by appropriate sacrifices and rituals. The occurrence of any negative event is blamed on spirits and rituals carried out to appease them.

These rituals many a times include animal sacrifices. For instance, to cure illness, the shaman called nyubu will assemble together a figure from straw, and while reading some spells over it, drain over it the blood of a sacrificed chicken. Once cured, the individual places this figure in the courtyard, of his or her home, where it is falls apart in due course. In case the disease is not cured, the individual is taken to the shaman, who lives some distance from the village, for a longer healing ritual and a possible exorcism.

The Apatani version of the land of the dead is neli, where all souls go after death. The corpses are buried on land owned by the deceased's family, and usually the grave is fenced and a garden is planted on it. In addition, a shrine is made of bamboo, its size determined by the wealth of the deceased. Animals are also sacrificed by the nyubu for the deceased's journey into neli, with the families of the rich offering expensive animals like the mithun (Indian bison) and pigs, while the poor offer smaller animals and birds, like chicken.

SOUTH INDIAN SHAMANS

Generally speaking, shamanism seems to have certain common characteristics across cultures and geographical areas, even if they are on opposite ends of the globe. These include an ability to move through realms of everyday reality to that of spirits, to use these journeys for healing and divination, an ability to communicate with spirits and exorcise them when necessary.

In several parts of India, variations of shamanistic practices are part of mainstream culture, such as the belief in spirit possession and the use of specialised exorcists, belief in powers of divination of a spirit medium, and so on. These are often associated with Tantra, rather than being identified with a separate shamanistic tradition. Tantra is a system of philosophy that has as its ultimate goal - the attainment of enlightenment.

Over time, there developed practices that took off from Tantric rites of sadhana and attempted to use them for shamanistic purposes—to attain 'siddhis' (powers), influence spirits, or gain worldly success, wealth and so on. Practitioners of the higher aspects of Tantra see this use of Tantra as a way of becoming further enmeshed in the material reality, rather than move towards a transcendence of it. Yet there is also an understanding that Tantric tools teach one to use and direct energy for one's goals, and for these, each individual must take responsibility.

Working with spirits is an ancient human endeavour, it would seem, given the fact that all around the world, it was one of the first wisdom traditions to emerge. Since then, whether overtly or in a hidden manner, it has remained part of our lives in some way, at least in places like India that have experienced a continuity of civilization, and where nothing was ever rooted out perforce, as happened with the wiccan and pagan cults in Europe.

In north India, there are shamanistic practitioners called ojha, who are often called in when spirit possession is suspected. There are also tantriks, who as outlined above, make the use of Tantric tools and methods to fulfil a range of needs that have nothing to do with the spiritual quest and that aspect of Tantra, such as providing charms to ensure spousal loyalty or male children, rituals to bring back to the fold a straying husband, and to enable success in academics, professions, businesses, and so on.

In south India, there exist some traditions of shamanism that are completely

Facing page: A shaman from the Apatani tribe of Arunachal Pradesh, nyubu, prepares to sacrifice a chick during a ritual for a recently deceased person. Nyubu shamans claim to be able to read the sacrificed animal's liver to determine the evil spirit responsible for a premature death.

Above and preceding pages: Theyyam dancers posing and performing the ritual dance. The Theyyam performer dresses up in the ornate costumes and headdresses associated with the deity being invoked, along with elaborate make-up. As he emerges in the garb of the deity, he looks at his face in a mirror. This action is said to bring the deity into his being, and the Theyyam begins in earnest.

unique in their practice, and are mostly used for the purposes of divination and healing. I will outline two of these here – Bhuta Kola of the Tulu-speaking community of Karnataka, and Theyyam of Kerala.

Bhuta Kola is the tradition of invoking and worshipping spirits, who are thought of as guardians, protectors and benefactors, through the agency of human mediums. These mediums play the role of the shaman, by inviting a particular spirit into his body, who then listens to the petitions placed before it and dispenses healing, divination of future circumstances, and even decisions on legal disputes. The writ of the spirits runs in the community, and decisions thus given are usually followed by all concerned. Perhaps part of the reason is fear of displeasing a spirit, who might then extract its pound of flesh through supernatural means.

The spirits are thus specific entities that came to be associated with a particular area or village over the years, and usually have background stories that explain the origin of this association. They could be animal spirits, like Pilichamundi who is a tiger spirit, or Annappa Panjurli, a boar, or they could be local heroes like Bobbaraya, the twin brothers Koti and Chennayya, Kalkuda-Kallurti, and so on. At times goddesses are also invoked. The spirits not only answer people's questions, they also might warn of impending danger and offer protection.

The Bhuta Kola ceremonies are organised regularly from November to May each year. A 'sthana' (place) is created for the invocation of the bhuta by marking out a triangle and creating a specific space under a tent put up for the occasion. The space is adorned with auspicious symbols, objects and offerings. The bhuta medium prepares for the ritual by adorning himself with the costume, headgear and make-up associated with the bhuta that is being invoked, donning feminine gear if the spirit is that of a woman. Each bhuta is distinguished by a different get-up, which the medium is familiar with.

As the medium enters the designated space, musicians begin playing drums and wind instruments, even as a female member of his family begins singing from the paad danaa, which detail the story of the particular spirit being invoked, and includes praises for the spirit's heroism, kindness, and so on. As the tempo builds up, the medium as if enters a trance, as the spirit takes over his body.

In this state, the spirit asks the reason for its invocation, which is explained by the organisers, who beg for its benevolence. The spirit might agree immediately and bless them and the gathering, or it might suggest some things that should be done for the wish to be fulfilled. At times, the spirit also chastises the community for something they might have done, or forgotten to do. After the ritual is over, the medium remembers nothing of it.

A tradition similar to Bhuta Kola is that of Theyyam, its name a corruption of the Sanskrit word 'devam', which means deity, and which is practised in parts of Kerala. In a caste-ridden society where the Brahmanas controlled access to the religious experience and were the keepers of sacred knowledge Theyyam was a way in which the masses could connect with the sacred dimension by bypassing Brahmanical control altogether. For, Theyyam could only be performed by members of tribal and so-called lower caste communities, with the performances being patronised by local landlords who considered it a way of assuring auspiciousness and the protection of the spirits.

Like Bhuta Kola, Theyyam is performed over a few months in the year, with the performers at times returning to other professions in the interim period. During the season of Theyyam, however, they are constantly on the move, from one village to another, where performances have been organised. Theyyam performers begin when they are young, and are usually trained by other male members of the family who might be senior performers. The trance, however, cannot be taught, and each performer must find access into it himself.

According to some estimates, there are a few hundred kinds of Theyyam, each to do with the invocation of a particular deity. For example, the Guligan Theyyam invokes Shiva, Vishnumurthi Theyyam invokes Vishnu, Bhagwati and Kali Theyyams invoke the goddess in these forms, and so on. It is performed in the open, usually in front of a shrine, and its duration can stretch from twelve to twenty-four hours.

As in Bhuta Kola, the performer dresses up in the ornate costumes and headdresses associated with the deity being invoked, along with elaborate make up. A short dance session, known as Thottam, has already been performed before

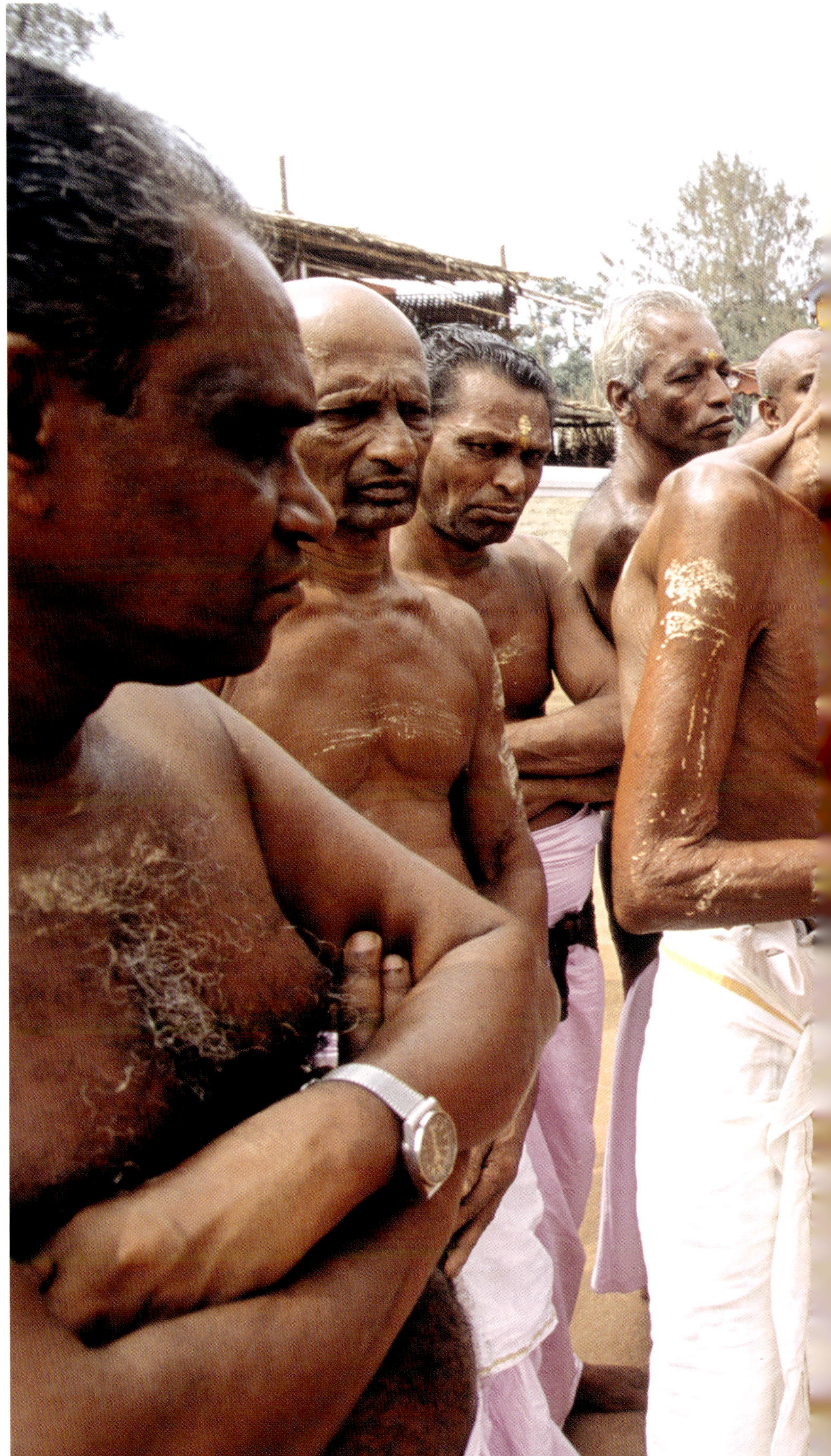

A Theyyam performer hands out the deity's blessings. During Theyyam, the deity seemingly comes alive and descends amongst devotees in the person of the performer, ready to listen to their woes and provide ready solutions and blessings. What is also significant is that caste Brahmanas touch the feet of low caste performers, levelling some of the hierarchy that otherwise governs society.

he gets dressed as the deity. Afterwards, as the performer emerges in the garb of the deity, he looks at his face in a mirror. This action is said to bring the deity into his being, and the Theyyam begins in earnest.

Most of the dance that now takes place is part of the process of the deity assuming its own identity within the dancer's body. Like the Bhuta Kola mediums, Theyyam dancers too do not remember anything about this period, when they became the deities they were impersonating. At times the deity might demand a sacrifice and imbibe blood, at other times he or she might partake of alcohol, offerings that are kept ready at the site.

As the deity becomes manifested, he or she invites questions and provides

answers, suggestions and advice. They might also be asked to bless children or newlywed couples, or cure an illness or ensure a job or a child. During Theyyam, the deity that is worshipped in the temple every day as if comes alive and descends amongst its devotees, ready to listen to their woes and provide ready solutions and blessings. What is also significant is that caste Brahmanas touch the feet of low caste performers, levelling some of the hierarchy that might otherwise govern society.

Shamanism, therefore, continues to impinge upon our modern, techno-savvy lives in the twenty-first century. Perhaps, we need to turn to it to understand dimensions of reality other than our own, and thus come to access a way of being that is more open, inclusive, and integrated.

A dramatic shot of a Theyyam dancer in the midst of a frenzied movement, as sparks fly from the fire that illuminates the scene. At this point, the dancer has become the deity, and will not be able to recall the events of the Theyyam later, as if he were indeed possessed for the time the performance lasted.

The Way of the Sufi

Sufism is held to be a mystical branch of Islam, the term *sufi* deriving from either *safa* meaning 'pure', or *suf*, meaning 'wool'. In all probability this has reference to the rough woollen clothes worn by the early Sufis. It may also be traced to the Greek word *sofia*, meaning 'wisdom'. Needless to say, all these interpretations make sense in the context of Sufism.

It is believed that Sufi teachings and practices were conveyed by the Prophet Mohammed, to a select group of students, who he felt might be suited to an exacting discipline of devotion and constant remembrance of God. Central to the Sufi way is an emphasis on the purification of oneself and cultivation of good qualities, in the hope getting closer to God.

A deep and abiding love for the Divine is expressed in most Sufi writings, in metaphors of human love, but used in the context of the soul's longing for the Divine, or the eternal beloved. The well known poetry of Rabia Basri and Mevlana Jalaluddin Rumi express this passion for God eloquently and movingly.

Sufi adherents lived a simple life, dedicated to the search for God. In this, they were not unlike the mendicants of the Indian subcontinent, who gave up worldly pursuits in the quest for transcendental truth. There are also several similarities between Sufi meditative techniques, yogic and Buddhist ones . During the Middle Ages, when most of them existed together, it is a matter of plain conjecture, that they might have borrowed from and even influenced one another. In India too where Sufism arrived in the twelfth century AD and became swiftly popular among the masses there was much intermingling of traditions, and adherents of one popular faith were often strongly influenced by another.

Though the initial Sufis were free spirits and operated

as solitary radicals, questioning the authority of the clergy, living like hermits and involved in their own spiritual search, as the movement grew and spread orders and centres of Sufis came to be established. Each order had its own set of teachings, rules and saints who they considered unique to their school. Some of these are Chishti, Naqshbandiyya, Shadhiliyya, Suhrawardi, Qadiri, Owaisi, Qalandariya, and so on.

In modern times, translations of Sufi poetry and teachings, and the emergence of liberal teachers willing to step out of traditional boundaries, has helped Sufism travel to new lands and peoples, much like Buddhism. There has been an effort to distil its core wisdom beyond the bindings of religion, which many feel have led to the distortion of Sufism. It must be said, however, that the beauty of Sufi poetry has done much to move the hearts of many, and convey the message of divine love in an age of materialistic grasping and greed.

From left to right: A Sufi musician in Istanbul in Turkey. Music and dance, frowned upon in orthodox Islam, became a part of the Sufi's way of connecting with the Divine; A group of Sufis whirling in Anatolia in Turkey. The act of whirling is a meditative one for the Sufi – centering the self, quieting the mind, and harmonising the individual with all of creation; A Sufi at the Sema Festival in Istanbul. The act of sema, or whirling, is the central practice of the Mevlevi order, which takes its inspiration from Mevlana Jalaluddin Rumi, the thirteenth century Sufi master.

All rights reserved. No part of this publication may be transmitted or reproduced in any form or by any means without prior permission from the publisher.

ISBN: 978-81-7436-864-5

© Roli & Janssen BV 2012

Published in India by Roli Books
in arrangement with Roli & Janssen BV
M-75, G.K. II Market, New Delhi-110 048, India.
Phone: ++91-11-29212271, 40682000
Fax: ++91-11-29217185
Email: info@rolibooks.com
Website: www.rolibooks.com

Editor: Aditi Ghosh
Design: Bonita Vaz-Shimray & Devan Das
Press-press: Jyoti Dey
Production: Naresh Nigam and Shaji Sahadevan

Printed and bound in Singapore

*

Photo credits

Bonita Vaz-Shimray: Page 112

Briana Blasko: Page 130

Corbis: Pages 1, 12-13, 14, 15, 21, 23, 26, 27, 28, 33, 36, 37, 38, 39, 42, 45, 50, 51, 52, 56-57, 58, 59, 60, 67, 71, 77, 78-79, 80-81, 82, 88, 89, 90-91, 92, 93, 108, 109, 110, 114-115, 117, 128, 129, 132, 134-135, 136, 138-139, 140-141, 143

Getty Images: Pages 6, 142, 11, 83

Roli Collection: Pages 2-3, 10, 43, 44, 54, 53, 55, 61, 62, 63, 114

Thomas Kelly: Pages 48-49, 84-85, 86, 87, 94-95, 96, 97, 98-99, 100-101, 102-103, 104, 105, 106, 107, 113, 118-119, 120, 121, 122, 125, 126-127

Vivek Desai: Pages 4, 8-9, 16, 17, 18-19, 20, 22, 24-25, 26, 29, 30-31, 32, 34, 35, 40-41, 46, 47, 64, 65, 68, 69, 70, 72-73, 74-75